Your Life:
An Owner's Guide

Your Life:
An Owner's Guide

Goals, Dreams, Values, Exercise,
Money and People

Michael R. Slavit, Ph.D.

ISBN: 1502995719
ISBN 13: 9781502995711
Library of Congress Control Number: 2014921353
CreateSpace Independent Publishing Platform
North Charleston, South Carolina

ACKNOWLEDGEMENTS

To my parents, Irma and Leonard Slavit, for their love and support.

To my sister Betsy for her love, support and skilled editing assistance.

To my sister Bobbie for her love and support.

To Dr. David J. Drum for years of guidance and assistance.

To Thomas DiSanto for technical assistance and guidance.

CONTENTS

                                                      page

Introduction xiii

I.   VALUES AND LIFE GOALS

    1. Values Clarification by the "Monster List" 3

    2. What is really important to you ? (Setting Major Life Priorities). 11

    3. Are you sure that is what you value most ?. 15

    4. Keeping Sight of Our Dreams 19

II.   MOTIVATION AND EMOTIONAL FACTORS

    5. The Anatomy of Motivation. 29

        Establishing a Goal· 30

Breaking Goals down into Achievable Steps · · · · 32
Overcoming External Barriers to
Goal Attainment · 34
Overcoming Internal Barriers to
Goal Attainment · 35
Seeking Help in Appropriate Ways · · · · · · · · · · 37
Anticipating future rewards · · · · · · · · · · · · · · · 39
The Motivation Paradox · · · · · · · · · · · · · · · · · 41

6. Coping with the Blues 44

Some Thoughts about the Blues · · · · · · · · · · · · · 44
The Road to Recovery · · · · · · · · · · · · · · · · · · 48
Getting out of a Slump · · · · · · · · · · · · · · · · · · 50

7. Practice Rational Thinking and Your Life
Will be Easier 54

Overcoming Self Defeating Thoughts · · · · · · · · 55
Rational Coping Thoughts · · · · · · · · · · · · · · · · 56

III.   MANAGING STRESS AND STRAIN

8. Your Experience of Stress and Strain 61

9. Constructive and Destructive Ways of Dealing with
Stress and Strain 65

10. Your Personal Habits 68

Nutrition · 68
Exercise · 71
Substances · 71
Sleep · .72

11. Physical Relaxation. 76

It really is biological, you know! · · · · · · · · · · · · · · 76
The Progressive Relaxation Exercise · · · · · · · · · · 78

Imagination: A Short Cut to Deep
Relaxation · 82
Train Yourself to Use Imagery · · · · · · · · · · · · · · 86

12. Recreation. 88

IV. TIME AND TASK MANAGEMENT

13. Manage Time and Tasks with Moderation ! 93

You can do it when you really want to · · · · · · · · · 93
What if I only need organization some
of the time ? · 94

14. How We set Ourselves up to Fail. 96

"I Can't Do It" · 96
"I Can't Imagine Doing It" · · · · · · · · · · · · · · · · · 98
Over-Committing Ourselves · · · · · · · · · · · · · · 101

15. Time and Task Management by Internal Review 103

16. Organizing Time 108

      How precious is your time? · · · · · · · · · · · · · · · 108
      What can you do with 5 minutes? · · · · · · · · · · · 109
      The Inevitable Lists and Calendars · · · · · · · · · 110

17. Relating to Others 113

      Encouraging Consideration · · · · · · · · · · · · · · · 114
      Assertive Communication Really Helps · · · · · · 117
      Relating to Others when Time & Productivity
      are at Stake Productivity are at Stake· · · · · · · · 121

V.   MATERIALS AND PHYSICAL ENVIRONMENT

18. Organizing Space 127

      Making our Work Space Suit Us · · · · · · · · · · · 127
      Contending with Paper· · · · · · · · · · · · · · · · · · 127

19. Making Housekeeping Tasks Easy. 130

      "Do Ten Things" · 130
      "Clutter Zones" are Okay· · · · · · · · · · · · · · · · · 131
      The "Nutcracker Suite" · · · · · · · · · · · · · · · · · 132

VI. PERSONAL FINANCE

20. Can money buy happiness? 137

      Is money important? · 137
      Is money the crucial factor in happiness? · · · · · · 137
      Are the best things in life really free? · · · · · · · · 138

21. Who is In Control? Are you? 141

22. Why Invest for the Future? 144

      Live for Today! (Right?) · · · · · · · · · · · · · · · · · · 144
      Retirement will not be easy! · · · · · · · · · · · · · · · 145

23. A Tale of Two Couples 148

24. Effective Cash Flow Management 157

      The Problem with Typical Budgeting · · · · · · · · 158
      "Regular" and Intermittent Expenses · · · · · · · · 158
      Picking out the Signal from the Noise · · · · · · · · 161
      The Cookie Jar Approach · · · · · · · · · · · · · · · · · 162

VII. EXERCISE

25. Overcoming Avoidance of Exercise 167

VIII. SOCIAL LIFE

26. Let Them Know You Think of Them ! 175

     Cards for All Occasions · · · · · · · · · · · · · · · · · · 175
     A Few Words of Caution in the Electronic Age 179

27. Entertaining in the Home 182

     Why does it seem so difficult? · · · · · · · · · · · · · · 182
     The Sunday Brunch · 184
     Theme Dinners with Shared
     Work and Expense · 185

APPENDICES

A. Stimulus Questionnaire · · · · · · · · · · · · · · · · · · 189

B. Birthdays, Anniversaries, etcetera · · · · · · · · · · · · 199

C. A Recipe for "Plebeian Night" · · · · · · · · · · · · · · 201

D. Glossary · 203

E. References · 215

INTRODUCTION

In today's world we face more questions than ever before about how to live effectively. This book will help you find answers to major questions such as "What values should I live by?" to intermediate questions such as "How can I manage anxiety and depressed mood?" to questions as small as "How can I keep the top of my desk uncluttered?" This book will neither preach to you nor tell you to change your basic lifestyle. You can choose to manage time, tasks, space, and events more effectively within practically any lifestyle you select. This book may change you forever. It will give you valuable insights along with the methods to put them to work for you. Once you are so equipped, you will not be able to resist making your life better.

In this day and age, people often need help to improve personal efficiency in practical ways as well as help with personal growth on an emotional level. Time management and personal budgeting are two examples of practical, strategic approaches. At a somewhat deeper level, some people need help to analyze their thoughts, work through their emotions, or examine their attitudes. At an even deeper psychological level, some need to gain insight into how they became the persons they are today by examining their values, motivations, and needs. All three levels are valid, helpful approaches when skillfully used.

Many people simply need help with the practical, strategic aspects of life and this book includes responses to that need. This volume is very much different from the ordinary self-help or time management book. Many approaches to self-help present "one suggestion fits all" methods. This book, on the other hand, offers a flexible program, presenting a variety of techniques, and placing those methods within a framework of individual values, goals, and personal styles. This book addresses both broad, philosophical aspects of lifestyle management and specific, nitty-gritty matters. The topics range from understanding values and long-term goals, to keeping sight of your dreams, to managing stress and anxiety, to managing time, managing money, maintaining an exercise regimen and keeping the top of your desk neat!

When I address "time and task management," I do so with methods designed to be more creative and permissive than typical scheduling approaches. For instance, I describe a method of management by internal review that you can use instead of written lists to keep track of your obligations. The method utilizes mental imagery, and many people find it to be a comfortable substitute for lists and calendars.

Another area I address is creative depression management. There is a point of view in which depression is seen as an inevitable part of the human condition (Kline, 1974). The high degree of stimulation and information processing we face in modern life may lead to occasional depression as a respite. Some individuals may be especially prone to occasional periods of withdrawal or low energy due to the high level of commitment and intensity of their daily lives. Occasional withdrawals may be extra distressing and disruptive for achievement-oriented individuals. In working with depressed clients, I have found a method that helps lower the frequency, depth, and duration of lowered energy states, and I have included a description of the method.

Another significant area included in this book is motivation. Although most people think of motivation as a single trait that is either present or not, this book will help the reader understand the components of effective motivation, and to learn to develop this important attribute.

If you choose to, you may use a stimulus questionnaire printed in Appendix A to give you an opportunity to begin the book with an increased awareness of your individual needs. This questionnaire is divided into eight sections that correspond to the eight sections of the book. They are entitled as follows:

1. Values and Life Goals
2. Motivation and other Emotional Factors
3. Stress and Strain
4. Time and Task Management
5. Materials and Physical Environment
6. Personal Finance
7. Exercise
8. Social and Family Life

This questionnaire may help you decide which of the various topics and chapters in the book are most important to you. Appendix F is a glossary of many of the words and phrases used in the text. Turn to this list of definitions for clarification of any terms unfamiliar to you.

Whether your concern is coping with stress, managing time, handling your money, enriching your social life, or keeping up with your exercise program, this book will help. Be patient and gentle with yourself and do not demand perfection. Read, think about the issues, and proceed in a comfortable manner.

Section I

Values and Life Goals

"Congruence" is a word that the late and famous psychologist Carl Rogers used to describe the compatibility of a person's inner experience and outward behavior. For you to live a congruent life, your goals will need to reflect **your** inner experience, not anyone else's. Competence and achievement are valued by many persons in our society, but this book will **not** advance the idea that you should structure your life to ensure optimum competence. While I do often identify productivity as one of five significant life goals, it is not my intention to promote the value that you "should" produce, produce, produce. I hope that this book will help you develop the awareness and methods to place productivity in its proper position in **your** value system, among other goals such as awareness, joy, meaning, and relationships. By helping you clarify the relative importance of your values, including productivity, I hope to enable you to achieve congruence of your values and behavior.

CHAPTER 1

VALUES CLARIFICATION BY THE "MONSTER LIST"

First of all, what is a value? We often use, and misuse, this word. A value is a principle, standard, or quality considered important or worthwhile. You could say, "My car is important to me." But is 'car' a value? No. "Car" is a **concrete noun**, and your car is not a value. Values are represented by **abstract nouns**. A car provides you with transportation, and this may give you a feeling of freedom. "Freedom" is an abstract noun, and is certainly a principle that may be valued.

The following values clarification method is an adaptation of a technique used by Steven D. Brown, Ph.D., former Director of the Counseling and Testing Center at the University of Georgia. This method is probably the most challenging, and also one of the most important, exercises in this book. Other exercises later on, rest assured, will seem easier. The exercise begins with the use of a large list - or "monster list" - of values.

On the next 2 pages you will see a list of 80 items that may be valued. Read this list, and after each item, rate the importance of that item to you, as follows:

"A"   Of high importance to you
"B"   Of moderate importance to you
"C"   Of little or no importance to you

accurate knowledge
advancement of society
ambition
beauty
competition
conquest
consistency
convenience
creativity
curiosity
discipline
economic security
emotional security
fairness
freedom from responsibility
freedom from restraint
happiness
helpfulness
humor
intellectual awareness
kindness
logic
loyalty
meaning
opportunism
patience
physical prowess
power

achievement
affection
austerity
comfort
competence
consideration
contentment
courage
cultural diversity
decadence
dominance
emotional health
excitement
faith
friendship
gentleness
health
honesty
independence
intimacy
lawfulness
love
material wealth
obedience
orderliness
physical activity
pleasure
prestige

productivity	prudence
rationality	respect for persons
respect for property	respect for values
responsibility	risk
self-discipline	self-improvement
self-sacrifice	sensory pleasure
sensory stimulation	sobriety
social interaction	spontaneity
striving	thrift
tradition	trust
variety	vitality
wealth	winning

After you have done this, count up the number of items that you have rated "A." It will be helpful for you to have a list of twenty to thirty values to work with. If you have given a rating of "A" to fewer than 20 items, look over your "B" list and promote enough of them to "B-plus" so that you will have 20 in your top group. If you have assigned a rating of "A" to more than 30 items, look them over and reduce enough of them to "A-minus" so that you will have cut your top list to 30. Make these choices carefully. Right away, you will have begun the process of clarifying your values.

The next step in this exercise is a challenging one. Write down your 20 to 30 highest values at the top of a blank sheet of paper. Drawing from the list of 20 or 30 values, make 3 or 4 lists of values that seem to fit together. Put values together in the same list when they seem to be part of a larger theme. Use each value only once. This may seem difficult, especially as a specific value may appear to you to belong equally to two lists. For the sake of clarity, confine each value to one list. These lists may represent major value themes in your life.

After you have created your 3 or 4 theme lists, your job is to label each list, then write a sentence that describes what each list says about what you want out of life. It may seem difficult to look at the items on each theme list and to distill them down to one or two sentences, but try it anyway. Taken together, these sentences will say a lot to you about your entire personal value system.

As an example, let me share with you the list of a former client. This is an actual list, but I will of course disguise the description of the individual, whom I will call Donald. Donald was a thirty-year-old college student when I worked with him. He was pursuing a degree in a technical field. He chose this field because he knew that this type of training would make him employable at a good salary. He came into counseling because he was feeling unmotivated and unfulfilled. The following are Donald's 29 highest rated values, arranged into four lists (Donald was unable to integrate them into three lists):

SOCIAL CONSCIENCE

advancement of society
consideration
cultural diversity
friendship
helpfulness
honesty
lawfulness
love
loyalty
obedience
respect for persons

respect for property
respect for values
responsibility
trust

PLEASANT LIFE

health
love
humor
friendship
social interaction
variety

PERSONAL DEVELOPMENT

courage
curiosity
emotional security
faith
intellectual awareness

ACHIEVEMENT

achievement
competence

Here are the sentences that Donald wrote for each of his four value theme areas:

SOCIAL CONSCIENCE: "I want to live in a good society…
a respectful, responsible, honest society."

PLEASANT LIFE: "I want my own personal existence to be a pleasant one. I want health, love, friendship, and fun."

PERSONAL DEVELOPMENT: "I want to be somewhat of an existentialist . . . I want to be always in the process of becoming better, through my curiosity and courage."

ACHIEVEMENT: "I have some sense of wanting competence and wanting to be responsible financially . . . but they are not as important as doing something beneficial for society."

You may already see what was causing Donald's lack of motivation and fulfillment. Here he was, studying for a degree that could bring him financial success. But social conscience is much higher than achievement in his scheme of personal values. Notice that a full FIFTEEN of Donald's highest values fell into the "social conscience" theme. There were only TWO under "achievement." Donald was facing a true dilemma. He had already committed himself to a technical degree. He was within a year of graduation, assuming that he could remain sufficiently motivated to pass. He was feeling a strong desire to do something of value for society in a more personal growth-oriented sense. He was not excited about a highly-paid occupation that did not seem as relevant to him in terms of his social conscience.

Donald's predicament probably reminds many readers of conflicts that they have faced themselves. What can we do when we find ourselves in a position in which we are not living according to our stated values?

There are three alternatives. First, we can change our behavior so that it is consistent with our values. Second, we can recognize that our true values are the ones exhibited by our behavior, and we can therefore stop paying lip service to values that are not truly ours.

Third, we can accept, at least temporarily, that our actions are not consistent with our values, and we can plan a course of action that will allow us to live in accordance with our values in the near future.

To Donald, the first choice meant that he would immediately have to give up his major in construction, and pursue training in teaching, social work, or journalism. He said that ideally he would have liked this choice, but that at age 30 he was already feeling that he was very late in getting into a career. In addition, he was aware that the alternative career choices would not afford him the income that the construction industry could.

As to choice two, Donald felt very strongly about his social conscience values. He was completely unwilling to abandon those values and to give up the view of himself that they represented.

Choice number three became a matter of considerable discussion. I made some tentative suggestions that were possible given the value he placed on frugality and his dislike of materialism. I suggested that if Donald were to work in the construction industry for three to five years, he might be able to afford a career shift later. If he were willing to maintain his current material standard of living, he would be able to save and invest much of his income from construction. If he were to make a change to a career with lower pay, he could supplement that pay with income drawn from his investments. The strength of this plan is that he would eventually be able to have both the satisfaction of working in a career consistent with his values, and a better income than that career would otherwise provide him. The weakness of the plan is that it would require him to put in three to five working years in a career incompatible with his stated values.

Donald decided, at least tentatively, on the third choice. This allowed him to plan to live more fully, in the future, in accordance with his values. It was an accommodation that he felt was reasonable and workable. He began to experience some renewed motivation, and a more positive feeling about his future.

When you have worked through this exercise for yourself, you may find that it gives you a new sense of clarity about your personal values. If your current lifestyle is consistent with these values, you will have reaffirmed that you are living in accordance with what is important to you. Some people, on the other hand, find that their values and lifestyle are in conflict. If you are among them, then you will be faced with the challenge of how to best resolve this conflict.

In general, resolving a conflict between our values and our actions can be done in one of three ways:

One. Make a change in your behavior so that you will be living according to your values

Two. Admit to yourself that the values that you have identified are not truly as important to you as the values served by your current lifestyle; or

Three. Continue with your current lifestyle, while making realistic plans to change it in the future so that you will then be living according to your values.

Be as gentle as you can with yourself if you do in fact discover that your life is not currently a reflection of your most strongly held values. Moreover, continue your reading of this book before making any final decisions or plans. The material in this book includes important information on motivation, goals, and effective task management. It will help you to implement any new plans you may wish to make.

◈

CHAPTER 2

WHAT IS REALLY IMPORTANT TO YOU ? (SETTING MAJOR LIFE PRIORITIES)

This exercise is a close adaptation of an exercise described in chapters 5 and 6 of Alan Lakein's book, *How to Get Control of Your Time and Your Life*, and is designed to help you re-examine your life goals and set them more firmly in your mind.

Assemble three sheets of paper. Allow your thoughts and fantasies to run freely. There is nothing indelible or permanent about this exercise. You are re-assessing priorities - **not signing a contract!**

For the next 3 to 5 minutes, write down all of your lifetime goals you can think of. You may list general goals, such as "happiness," or specific goals such as "walking the entire Appalachian Trail." Write down whatever comes into your mind. Next, take an additional 2 to 3 minutes to re-state three of these life goals. You may want to amend or combine some of your goals. For instance, if you listed among your life goals:

      1. happiness and contentment,
      2. building a home, and
      3. living in the mountains;

you may want to restate a goal such as: "Building a home in the mountains and living peacefully there." Now that you have a set of three life goals to **consider**, **pursue**, **revise**, or **abandon**; take a **second sheet** of paper and take 3 to 5 minutes to list things you would like to do during the next 5 years. Again, let your imagination roam freely, and do not censor your responses. Now, as with the life goals, spend another 2 to 3 minutes picking out and re-stating three of these goals. Next, take your **third sheet** of paper. Use your imagination, and imagine as vividly as you can that you have 6 months to live. Imagine you have an incurable condition that will not cause you any loss health or abilities, but from which you will suddenly expire in 6 months. All final planning, such as wills, burial arrangements, and financial arrangements for your family are complete. Spend 2 or 3 minutes writing down the things you are going to do for the next 6 months.

Finally, spend a few minutes looking over your lifetime, 5-year, and 6-month goals. Remembering that you may re-arrange, edit, or completely revamp these goals whenever you wish, consider ways in which your short and long-term goals are consistent or inconsistent with one another.

There will probably be some major differences for most responsible persons. After all, if you had only 6 months to live, you would no longer have to be concerned with your education, career, or retirement planning. However, if your answers to the 6-month question are **dramatically** different from your 5-year and lifetime goals, you may have a goal conflict, and it will be in your interest to do some thinking about these issues.

Often, persons completing this exercise list lifetime and 5-year goals that involve investments and achievements. Their 6-month goals are often focused in areas such as recreation, personal fulfillment and relating to loved ones. It is understandable and proper that this is so, to some extent. After all, the conditions described in the exercise were:

> "You have an incurable condition that will not cause you any loss health or abilities, but from which you will suddenly expire in 6 months. All final planning, such as wills, burial arrangements, and financial arrangements for your family are complete."

Therefore, it is natural that many of us would turn away from our life projects and plan activities that would be more immediately gratifying. However, I believe this warrants further analysis. First, if there are activities and relationships that would command our attention were we to have only six months left, then we are telling ourselves that we value those activities and relationships highly. One question is: Can we pursue other activities and live with full vitality, purpose, and commitment if we are not currently paying sufficient attention those we most highly value? The next questions are: What level of attention to the highly valued activities is "sufficient"? and What level of attention to the highly valued activities is achievable?

If such an apparent conflict exists between what you would really like to be doing, and what you are choosing to work toward based on your assessment of the reality of your situation, you may find the following example comforting.

I have a friend who expressed an ambition to have a 42-foot ocean-going sailboat, and to live on the boat, sailing from place to place. When my friend examined his current finances, family obligations, and the demands of his profession, he became despondent because he could not envision making any progress whatsoever toward his ambition. I suggested that he make a small commitment of time and money on a regular basis toward the goal. For instance he could, with limited time and funds, subscribe to and read a yachting magazine, take a course in navigation, go to shops or yard sales near the ocean to buy a few pieces of hardware that might be useful in the future, and do a small amount of woodworking to keep sharp the skills that would be needed to build, rebuild, or repair his dream vessel. Doing these things would not hinder his ability to pursue his immediate obligations. They would have some present value, and they would help to keep the dream alive and provide progress toward it. My friend responded quite favorably. He felt released from what he had seen as an unresolvable conflict between long and short-term goals.

Working toward both short and long-term goals is a key concept in gaining control of our lives. We can spend a major amount of our time and effort on tasks that seem immediate or continuous, but we can also make distinct steps toward long-range goals. By doing so, we may be able to live with increased vitality and purpose. And, perhaps even more importantly, we may retain an important part of our self-definition.

CHAPTER 3

ARE YOU SURE THAT IS WHAT YOU VALUE MOST ?

Here is another exercise to raise your consciousness about your priorities. The process is called role stripping. First, list the seven most important roles that you occupy in your life. (Example: son, friend, student, lover, carpenter, neighbor, soft-ball team member, protégé, mentor, brother). Your next task is to choose two roles to drop. Then, imagine explaining your choices to a friend or confidant. If you are going through this book with a partner, explain these choices to one another. In actuality, although it is inevitable that we relegate roles to a low priority status relative to other roles, a role does not often need to be dropped entirely. However, in order to achieve **as much values clarity as possible**, imagine having to drop the two roles **entirely**.

After you have imagined describing your reasons for dropping two roles, the next task will be for you to choose two additional roles to drop, and to imagine explaining those choices to a friend or confidant.

Elena's account may illustrate the value of this exercise:

> My life used to feel very burdensome much of the time. It still does to some extent, because I am a very

conscientious person with high standards for myself. However, I have learned to let go of some of my self demands since I used the role-stripping exercise to get a better understanding of my priorities.

When I was asked to list my seven most important roles, I listed the following:

1. mother
2. wife
3. daughter
4. teacher
5. friend
6. neighbor
7. community organizer

I take all these roles seriously, and I hesitated when I was asked to choose two roles to drop. I do not want to drop any of these roles! I did realize that the demands on my time and energy were wearing me thin, so I went along with the exercise. The first two roles I chose to drop were community organizer and neighbor. It was hard for me to imagine dropping these roles. By "community organizer", I am referring to activities such as helping to organize a neighborhood crime watch, serving on committees of the Parent/Teachers Organization, and involvement in local politics. By "neighbor", I mean being available to my neighbors to help when needed, to socialize, and just to help make the neighborhood a friendly place to live.

I did not, and still do not, want to drop those roles. However, for the sake of clarity, I imagined dropping the two. After all, my roles as mother, wife, and daughter are my strongest and most intimate family ties. In addition, I have some close longtime friends who are very close to me, and my profession as a teacher is obviously important to me for both monetary and personal reasons. Therefore, "community organizer" and "neighbor" were dropped.

Next, I was asked to drop two of the remaining five, and I really became uncomfortable. Just thinking about giving up my roles as friend and teacher was unnerving, but giving up my roles as mother, wife, and daughter was unthinkable. So, I dropped the roles of friend and teacher, leaving mother, wife, and daughter.

Obviously, ever since I did this exercise I have not actually had to drop any of the seven roles. However, having gone through the exercise, I am much clearer about my priorities, and much better able to handle conflicting demands on my time and energy. I am giving less time to some of the roles that I imagined dropping during the exercise. The seven roles are now organized, in my mind, in three levels of priority:

        A. mother, wife, daughter
        B. friend, teacher
        C. neighbor, community organizer

If I am working on a community project and I find out that my parents need me, I cut my project work short and attend to my parents. I may even resign from the task and ask that it be assigned to someone else. I used to feel frustrated, and sometimes even resentful, toward my parents for taking my attention away from an important community project. I still feel somewhat frustrated if I have to abandon my goal of doing a great job on a community project, but I know where my priorities are. I make the adjustment with far less difficulty than I used to. I enjoy my sense of clarity and the comfort and flexibility it gives me!

Having completed the exercises concerning priorities prescribed in this chapter, you may have heightened your awareness of life alternatives and, if successful, will have achieved more clarity in your evaluation of your choices.

CHAPTER 4

KEEPING SIGHT OF OUR DREAMS

I have come to believe that this chapter of the book is one of the most important. How many of us have long-term goals or dreams toward which we are making no progress? Have we actually begun to lose sight of that dream? The real issue for us, if we are among the many persons who admit to feeling that we are losing sight of such a dream or goal, is not simply loss of goal attainment. **The problem is one of self-definition.** In the discussion following the exercise on long term, intermediate term, and immediate goals, I told you about my friend who had become depressed because he was not making progress toward his dream of owning a 42-foot ocean-going sailboat and leaving his job for adventure on the high seas. This is an actual person and not an hypothetical friend, and I had helped this individual to overcome his depression by suggesting small, achievable, interim steps toward the dream. Not incidentally, this individual now owns a 21-foot sailboat, and hopes to "trade up" to a 25-foot boat soon. He no longer feels immobilized in pursuit of his dream, and now feels his life is more vital and purposeful.

I am sure that many of us, if not most, have goals or dreams on which we are not making any progress. I am going to give some ideas about some of the effects of goals and dreams on our personal effectiveness, our daily lives, and our self-image. I will be promoting the point of view that an appropriate approach to our long-term goals and dreams can enhance our lives, and I will be addressing the following questions:

- Does it matter if our dreams are realistic?
- Will attention to a dream detract from our ability to deal with our daily lives?
- Are our dreams and our self-image related?
- What if our dreams seem so unattainable that we feel stalled?
- Should we even have such dreams?

Let us address the issue of whether or not our dreams are realistic. Some people may have dreams that seem grandiose or unattainable. Others may have dreams that do not appear to be as far-fetched. For instance, some may dream about being a movie star, a star athlete, or a successful national statesman. Others may dream about writing a book, building a home, or raising a prize bull.

It does matter whether our dreams are realistic, but we have to be very careful about what we say is realistic and what is not. If a thirty-year-old person who is **not** in excellent physical condition dreams about being an Olympic athlete, that is clearly **not** realistic. If a person of average intelligence dreams of becoming a famous research physicist, it is **not** realistic. However, as long as a dream is not clearly outside our physical or intellectual limits then, although it may be very improbable, it is not necessarily unrealistic.

One other question that I am often asked is whether I believe that working on small steps toward a long-term dream enhances or diminishes a person's ability to devote sufficient attention to his or her daily responsibilities. This probably varies a great deal from one person to the next. When pressed to give an opinion, I state that working toward our dreams energizes us, and that it therefore enhances the ability of the average person to handle daily routine tasks.

Even an improbable dream may be effectively pursued with psychological benefit to the individual. For instance, imagine that a woman with a high school diploma who is married, of moderate financial means and employed at home with two children, dreams of having a college degree. You may think that attaining a college degree is improbable, given the constraints of time and money. Perhaps it is improbable, but it is not unrealistic. Let us examine some realistic initial steps a person in this situation could take. Her first step might be to find out about evening college classes. Her next step might be to arrange for childcare two nights per week so she can attend classes. A third step might be to find out about financial aid and, if it is unavailable, to save enough money to pay for one course. A fourth step might be to register for and take one course. Passing one course does not equal a college degree, but it is progress, and progress tends to lead to more progress. Even more importantly, while gradually building up her college credits, this person is thinking of herself not as a person stuck in one role, but rather **as a person on her way toward attaining a college degree. Her self-definition is changed**. Yes, it is possible that her college studies could take time away from her family obligations.

> **However, it is also possible that her increased self-esteem could give her increased energy and motivation to deal with her obligations to her home and family.**

Some people suggest that it can be dangerous for a person to maintain improbable dreams. They ask whether such dreams could make them frustrated, and take their attention away from the parts of their life that need immediate attention. Of course if people spend a lot of time daydreaming, it could take their attention away from their home, job, and family, without putting anything productive into their lives. Therefore, I do not promote long, useless daydreams, but I promote another point of view about personal goals and dreams.

The issue is not goal attainment, but self-definition. The individual described earlier had not merely decided that his goal was to live on and sail a 42-foot boat; he had begun to **define himself** as a person who would someday own, live on, and sail such a craft. He had been defining himself as an adventurer. When he became depressed over the lack of progress, **his depression was more a loss of self than a loss of an achievement**. It is **because** we may define ourselves in terms of our dreams that it **is** so very important to attend to the issue of our dreams.

Several years ago when I was leading a four-session group called "Enhancing Control of Your Lifestyle and Workstyle," a twenty-eight year old student who had returned to college as an undergraduate reacted very strongly to the question about losing sight of dreams. He went on to say that he had always dreamed he would build himself a log cabin home from a kit, and would live in it. He stated that he was beginning to wonder whether he would **ever** attain this goal, and that he did indeed feel that he had defined himself as a person who would build a log cabin, and that he felt that he was in some way losing himself.

I asked Ted (not his real name) how much time he now had to work on his dream, and he replied that his priority was now to complete school and that he had no time at all for this pursuit. I replied that I did not believe this to be true, and asked if he could spare one week-end per month for his project. He agreed that he had that much time to spare, but could not imagine how one weekend per month could help. Ted had already stated that he knew of three companies in North Carolina, within six hours driving distance, which sold the log cabin kits in which he was interested. He could plan one weekend per month to take a trip to North Carolina. I suggested that he could set up appointments in advance to spend time with sales representatives or customer service consultants of the companies in question. I suggested that he could ask to be shown log cabins that had been built from their kits, and that he could ask specific questions about such matters as land requirements, foundations, skills needed to complete the plumbing and electrical systems, heating and ventilation, et cetera. Once he had this information, he could go about acquiring the knowledge and skills that he lacked. Many community colleges offer building trades courses that require a five or six hour per week time commitment, which Ted could afford to make, at least one semester or quarter per year. Ted began to understand that he could indeed keep sight of his dream of building a log cabin, and therefore maintain his definition of himself as a person who would someday build such a home. He could do so with a manageable time commitment. He became rather excited about the project.

> I told Ted that in my opinion it was not as important that he ever build a log cabin as it is that he overcomes his feelings of being immobilized, and that it was important that he maintain his self-definition.

That is my main point in writing this part of the book: to help individuals to keep their dreams in sight, to feel purposeful rather than immobilized, and to maintain parts of their self-definition that have become important to them.

It is very important to avoid the sense of being immobilized. It is appropriate to go slowly at our endeavors, but stopping is likely to be psychologically destructive. Purposeful, vital, committed living depends on avoiding a sense of immobilization, and on exercising our ability to take steps toward our dreams. To exercise these abilities, people may have to train themselves to be more methodical and systematic. My hope is that this book will be a significant resource to many persons for this purpose.

What if someone just says, "I don't want to bother with goals and dreams. I just want to take it easy and be satisfied with who I am and with what I've got"? That may be fine. Some people seem to find solace and comfort in finding a niche for themselves and settling into a routine without dreaming about making their lives any different. Some people alternate periods of growth and of working toward dreams with periods of rest, routine, and not rocking the boat. There is no right or wrong in this. I have no belief that people "should" pursue long-term goals. However, some people do have dreams and do not want to surrender them. It is possible to find a way to keep the dream alive in a way that does **not** interfere with daily life and responsibilities, but that **does** help maintain self-image. It is possible to feel vital and alive and to feel the sense of always becoming someone just a little better -- someone a little more fulfilled.

In summary, consider the following points:

> 1. To some extent, self-image may be tied up with a dream. There may be a productive way to maintain and enhance that self-image.

> 2. Take small steps toward a dream. Avoid the sense of being immobilized.

3. We would never attain, invent, or discover anything valuable if we shied away from improbable dreams, though truly unrealistic dreams are not helpful.

4. We can make progress toward a long-term dream without detracting from our ability to deal with our daily lives. In fact, we may find increased energy for our routine tasks and obligations.

5. To pursue or not to pursue goals and dreams is a matter of personal choice . . . a choice you may confirm or change at will.

Section II

Motivation and Emotional Factors

CHAPTER 5

THE ANATOMY OF MOTIVATION

Everyone has desires and dreams. We have ideas about what would be a happy, satisfying life. In most cases, we have explored some of our dreams. Subconsciously we may have created an entire set of images portraying them. Moreover, many individuals have specific goals that they have set for themselves in order to try to spur themselves on toward their dreams.

Despite the existence of desires, goals, and dreams, a large percentage of people find themselves failing to put a great deal of effort into the pursuit of their goals and dreams. In effect, they appear to lack the motivation to succeed. Just what is this sometimes-elusive commodity ... "motivation"?

Although in one sense, you may be motivated to succeed, in another sense you may lack **effective motivation**. Plain motivation means just wanting to succeed. Effective motivation means being in the habit of addressing your obligations in certain ways - ways that will result in the following components being present in your plans:

1. **Establishment of a goal**
2. **Breaking the goal down into smaller, achievable steps**
3. **Overcoming external blocks to goal - attainment**
4. **Overcoming internal blocks to goal - attainment**
5. **Seeking help in appropriate ways**
6. **Anticipating future rewards**

When you are able to plan things in this way - and to **explicitly** and **unambiguously** address these 6 components of effective motivation - you will find yourself accomplishing more.

Component #1
Establishing a Goal

It is not enough to have ideas on what a happy, satisfying life would be. And, it is not enough to have a set of images that portray those ideas. Most individuals need to be more specific in their thinking and planning in order to be effectively motivated.

In Chapters 1 through 4, we discussed values and priorities. In order for our goals to be suitable for us, those goals need to be consistent with who we are at the most basic level - consistent with our personal value system. Review those chapters and the exercises contained within them if you are having any difficulty in settling on a goal to pursue.

When you select a goal, be sure that it is specific and definite enough for you to know when you have achieved it. The following are two lists - the first of indefinite goals and the second of the same goals stated in definite terms:

Indefinite Goals
1. I want to improve my grades in school.
2. I want to save some money for emergencies.
3. I want to "get in shape."
4. I want to gain some added skills to enhance my employability.
5. I want to improve my relationship with my brother.

Definite Goals
1. I will to bring my grade point average up from 2.7 to 3.5 by the end of Fall quarter next year.
2. I will economize on entertainment and clothing purchases, and will save at least $100 per month until I have $1,000 set aside for emergencies.
3. I will begin walking two miles, three times per week. Within 2 months, I will begin running and, within 6 months, I will be running 3 miles in 24 minutes or less.
4. I will purchase a spreadsheet program for my computer. I will pick out a set of data that I am sufficiently interested in to have fun with, so that I will enjoy learning the spreadsheet program. Then I will devise some problems to solve until I have become proficient enough with the program to legitimately list it on my resume.
5. I will ask my brother to set a number of occasions for us to get together for recreation and to talk. I will help him to understand both the cause some of my resentments from the past, and my desire that we have a closer relationship now. When we can express genuine feelings to one another without fear of having those feelings used against us, we will have achieved a major improvement in our relationship.

Make your goals specific enough for you to know when you have achieved them. And, set them at a reasonable difficulty level. Goals should be sufficiently challenging to be meaningful, but not so difficult as to be unattainable or frustrating.

Component #2
Breaking Goals down into Achievable Steps

This may be the most important component of effective motivation. When we look at a task as a whole, it may seem so formidable or complicated that we may back down from it. We may feel incapable of accomplishing it. At that moment, we are in danger of abandoning that task in despair before we have begun.

However, if we can break the larger goal down into smaller sections, then we no longer have to confront the entire task. We need only address the first step. The task no longer appears overwhelming. We may complete the first step successfully and experience feelings of accomplishment. This gives us energy for handling the second step, and so on. The entire process of task completion and goal attainment depends on getting started, and getting started very often depends on setting up an achievable, non-formidable first step.

Examples of Setting up the First Few Achievable
Steps of a Larger Task

1. Suppose you have a term paper to write. The entire task, including selecting a topic, doing some background reading, deciding on a focused aspect of the topic to write about, creating an outline, writing a first draft, et cetera, may seem overwhelming. To cut this job down to size, here are a few possible initial steps:

> **One**. Tentatively decide on a topic, and go to the library to find where books on that topic are shelved.
> **Two.** Go to that section of the stacks, and pull out several books, one at a time. Leaf through them.

Read the table of contents. Go to a chapter or two and read a few paragraphs to determine if the author's style is readable for you.

Three. Select a few of these books to borrow and to read later.

Steps one, two and three could take you from a half-hour to an hour. Completing these steps will not complete your paper. However, if you perform them you will have overcome immobility and you will have made a start.

2. Suppose you are moving to a new apartment and have to pack. The entire task, including acquiring cardboard boxes, discarding belongings you no longer need, disassembling stereos and furniture, arranging for final utility bills, et cetera, may be awful to contemplate. Try these few initial steps:

> **a.** Make a few trips to supermarkets, package stores or other sources for cardboard boxes and collect a supply.
> **b.** Make a list of categories of your belongings, for example kitchen supplies, clothing, decorative items, cosmetics. One category at a time, go through these belongings and set aside those you will discard or donate. Take them away.
> **c.** Beginning with those items you will keep but that you use least often, pack belongings into boxes. Make lists of contents and label the boxes and the lists with matching letters or numbers.
> **d.** Make up a form letter that includes the date of your move and your new address. Leave a space for the name and address of the person or agency whom you must inform. Make enough copies to enable

you to write to every utility, magazine, credit card, et cetera, with whom you do business.

Steps a, b, c, and d could take you from one to several hours over the period of a few days. Completing these steps will not complete your packing and moving, but you will have made a great beginning!

Component #3
Overcoming External Barriers to Goal Attainment

The road to goal attainment is strewn with obstacles. Some are of our own making, but many are not. There are external forces or factors that we must successfully negotiate if we are to succeed. These obstacles come in a great variety. They may be forces of nature, human laws or rules, other people's competing wishes, or actual physical obstacles. Whatever their nature, it is important that you be able to identify them and plan to contend with them. Neglecting to do so could result in frustrated plans that can lower that commodity we are discussing - motivation.

The following are two examples of overcoming external blocks to goal attainment:

1. Maria had always wanted to grow her own vegetables. She bought a house with what appeared to be a fine garden spot. However, she soon found out that her land was midway between higher and lower ground, and that when there was heavy rain the run-off would wash out her garden. Then she purchased some railroad ties and placed them on the high side of her garden spot. On each end of her barrier, she dug trenches from her property to the lower ground, filling the trenches with gravel. From then on, when

it would rain heavily, the run-off water would at first pool behind her railroad ties, and flow into the trenches. The combination of heavy rain and the unfortunate placement of her garden spot was the external barrier that Maria overcame by creative landscaping.

2.   Ralph wanted to open his own restaurant. He had a three-story house one block from a busy commercial street. Unfortunately, his property was zoned for residential use and the neighbors were not happy with the idea of a commercial establishment near them. Ralph talked with his neighbors and, to enlist their support, promised to plant thick evergreen shrubbery to act as a barrier between his parking lot and the adjoining properties. The residential zoning and the neighbors' anxieties were an external block to goal-attainment, but Ralph was able to successfully petition for a zoning variance by easing his neighbors' fears.

External blocks will often be present to at least some degree in situations when you strive to attain meaningful goals. Identifying those barriers as soon as possible, and making explicit plans to overcome them, will be an important part of your effective motivation.

Component #4
Overcoming Internal Barriers to Goal Attainment

The road to goal attainment is laden with obstacles, and some we create. To overcome these obstacles we need to identify them and describe them in a manner that makes them manageable. For instance, if I label myself "lazy," I create an obstacle by implying I am and always will be lazy in all situations. This is probably not true. Perhaps a more accurate statement is "When I cannot clearly imagine how to attain my goal, I stop working hard, and this gives the appearance of laziness." The internal block to be overcome in such an instance, then, would **not** be "laziness," but rather "a tendency to stop working when goal-attainment cannot be imagined." A plan can be made for overcoming **that** obstacle. We can learn to create vivid images of goal-attainment, and we can remind ourselves to review those images now and then during our work. However, if we thought of the obstacle as the trait of laziness, then no concrete plans for resolving that problem could be made.

The following are two examples of overcoming internal blocks to goal attainment:

1. Sam was a state employee with a steady income, but he felt unfulfilled in his work. He felt no sense of purpose or meaning in his work, and he would feel depressed. Sam had an idea for a business venture. He had talked over his plan with a number of business professionals who told him his idea was feasible. However, failure in operating a business is always a possibility, and Sam found himself dwelling on the possibility of failure, and on the terrible disruption and humiliation he was sure he would experience if he gave up a secure income for a business that later failed.

Finally, Sam thought through in specific terms just what a business failure would entail. When he took apart his fears and examined them in the light of day, he realized that although a business failure would be a disappointment and a true inconvenience, it would not be the end of the world, of his career, or of his ability to continue to support himself. Sam's overblown fears of failure were the internal block to his goal-attainment. He overcame those fears by examining them specifically and rationally.

2. Debra wanted to be a dancer. However, her father was a geologist and her mother was an oceanographer, and both parents

wanted her to follow their footsteps into the sciences. Debra tried enrolling in a dance school, but was so distracted by the feeling that she was letting her parents down that she could not succeed. Finally, she thought through the situation. She respected her parents' right to have their hopes for her. However, she had the conviction that a parent brings a child into the world so that the child can develop his or her potential – not to live up to parental dream. She wanted her parents to allow her to follow her own path and her own dreams. When she had examined the situation and had decided philosophically that her own desires for herself superseded her parents' hopes for her, she was able to pursue dance with renewed vigor and concentration.

Debra's guilt feelings were her internal block to goal attainment. She overcame this block through a philosophical examination of the relative importance of children's and parents' wishes.

Component #5
Seeking Help in Appropriate Ways

Actually, component #5 is often practiced in conjunction with the other components, particularly 3 and 4. The examples I gave of persons overcoming external and internal blocks to goal-attainment were written without any explicit mention of seeking help from others, whereas in many actual situations overcoming barriers results from a combination of self-help and assistance from others.

Seeking help can be a difficult process for many individuals in our society. Many persons have a tendency toward counterdependence. That is, they have no difficulty offering help **to** others, but feel very awkward about seeking or accepting assistance **from** others. This can be a very sad thing for them. We can experience a very satisfying feeling of human closeness and support when we accept help from others, but some people miss out on this feeling.

From a practical point of view, the total knowledge, skills, and experience needed to successfully negotiate this world is formidable. A reluctance to seek help from others when appropriate can be a significant handicap to effective goal-attainment.

The following is an example of seeking help for purposes of goal attainment:

Linda had grown up with no knowledge or skills in building things or working with tools. She felt that this was a gap in her personal repertoire, and she wanted the skills to build or repair pieces of furniture, porch railings on her home, et cetera. She set a goal for herself of purchasing some tools, setting up a workshop in her garage, and acquiring some building skills.

As a first step toward achieving her goal she sold and donated unused possessions that were taking up the needed space in her garage. An external block to goal attainment was the lack of electrical outlets in her garage for lighting, portable heaters and fans, and power tools. She hired an electrician to install the needed outlets. Her internal block to goal attainment was that she could not determine what tools to buy, and she could not overcome her immobilization. Linda was not asking for help because she was afraid of appearing dependent and stupid.

Finally, she discussed her dilemma with two friends who were woodworking hobbyists. She invited them for lunch, telling them that she would appreciate a few hours of specific tips on how to set up her workshop, what tools to purchase, and how to get going. She told them that she believed she would appear stupid but that she really needed help to get started. After receiving her friends' help, Linda bought the tools they had recommended. One friend visited and helped her assemble a workbench, and within a few months Linda had built a bookcase, had made a small home repair, was experiencing a new sense of competence, and was feeling great about herself. Requesting help from her friends was a crucial step in enabling Linda to attain her goal. It was the turning point of her effective motivation.

Component #6
Anticipating future rewards

Many goals that people set for themselves are long term. Therefore, an important component of effective motivation is maintaining drive and enthusiasm over the long haul. It is not unusual for a person to set a goal and work hard, only to languish somewhere along the way and to leave the goal unreached. This is probably true more often than not.

All five of the previously discussed components are important, with special emphasis on component #2 - breaking the goal down into smaller, achievable steps. But even after seeking help when appropriate, overcoming external and internal barriers to goal-attainment, and achieving steps toward the goal, the human motivational apparatus can still break down. The final ingredient is to occasionally remind yourself of the ultimate goal of your efforts. Try not to spend so much time imagining the future that you waste valuable time. But do occasionally bring to mind an image of goal attainment and its rewards.

Many of my clients over the years have been college students, whose goals include completing school and getting a good job. Completing college is certainly a long-term goal. But many students want their college degree yesterday, and they try to take as many credit hours as they can every quarter or semester in order to get it over with. I often found myself using an athletic analogy, and telling a student:

> College is a distance event, not a sprint. In a sprint, you can run into oxygen debt, because the event will be over in such a short time. But in a distance event you cannot run into oxygen debt. You must stay within your abilities and set a pace you can maintain.

Part of staying within our abilities is pausing now and again to reward ourselves for progress. For many individuals the reward may be an intrinsic one. That is, the task completion itself may be so rewarding that no extrinsic reward is needed. Other persons need to set up a reward system for themselves. When they have completed a step toward their goal, they need to allow themselves an activity, a gift for themselves, or just time to relax. What to use as a reward is very much a matter of personal choice. I have found that time for a pleasant activity works well as a reward for many adults, since time for recreational pursuits is the very item that may be sacrificed while actually working on the tasks.

I will offer one admonition. It would probably be best if the reward does not by its very nature cause backsliding on the goal. For instance, if your goal is to reduce your weight from 180 pounds to 140 pounds, a hot fudge sundae after each 5-pound loss might not be the best choice as a reward!

I have described the six components of effective motivation, and I now offer an idea for making these components part of your internal machinery rather than leaving them as pages in this book.

I suggest that you take a few minutes two or three times a week to write a short story. I am suggesting a **very short story**, and literary excellence is irrelevant.

You have undoubtedly had the experience of reading a story or seeing a movie or a television show, and of identifying with a character in the story. You know you are identifying with a character when that person does something and you find yourself thinking "No, don't do that!!" When you experience this, make a mental note of it. Then as soon as you have a chance, sit down and write a brief story about that character. One-half page to one page will probably suffice. The key is to include in your brief story a description of your character using the six components of effective motivation. When you have trained yourself to write brief stories that clearly and unambiguously include the six components of effective motivation, those ideas will begin to sink into your unconscious as well as your conscious thoughts, and you will find yourself being a more effectively motivated person. It will require a conscious act of will on your part to discipline yourself to perform this exercise two or three times a week for several weeks. It will be worth it! Do it!

The Motivation Paradox

Performance goes up as our level of arousal goes up . . . . to a point. Then, performance drops as arousal gets even higher. This phenomenon is known as the Yerkes-Dodson Law, and it has profound implications for us as we attempt to raise our efficiency and performance. The Yerkes-Dodson Law is typically described as a curve – like the top half of a circle.

According to the motivation curve, performance is very low when we are asleep or bored, and climbs to its highest point when we are at optimal arousal. However, as arousal, or motivation, continues to increase, performance drops. We get into a danger zone in which anxiety, high anxiety, and rigid self-demands actually decrease our performance. This is a difficult pill to swallow for most persons in our society, who tend to believe that we can drive ourselves to peak performance through rigid self-demands, and by being our own worst critic.

Search your memory and your experiences for a particular type of event that may convince you of the truth of the motivation curve. Have you ever practiced a skill that you sometimes performed at a function in front of an audience? Examples may include playing a musical instrument, being on a debating team, or playing athletics. (When I give lectures on this topic approximately eighty percent of the audience - males and females - typically answer affirmatively). As an example, have you ever played an athletic activity such as softball at a picnic, at which no team standings were at stake? (Again, about eighty percent usually say "yes.") Now ... have you ever noticed that while performing a skill in a relaxing setting with nothing at stake, you found yourself doing your very best? (Almost the entire eighty percent typically say that in fact they have found themselves being their very most artful and skillful while performing at the relaxing event). This is a paradox. The less we tell ourselves that we "have to succeed," the more success we are likely to achieve.

What does this mean? Clearly, when there is something at stake or you are playing to win, your motivation is very high. You are, in effect, highly aroused, but your performance may suffer. You can actually see how performance declines for many people when they are highly aroused. There is a visible physical tightness that works against their most artful performance.

**But why do you perform so well when nothing is at stake?
Because <u>you</u> <u>love</u> <u>it</u> ... that's why ! ! !**

You love doing your best! It is intrinsically satisfying to experience a peak performance. This is true for almost all persons, whether the performance is artistic, athletic, social, vocational, or academic. And that's all the motivation you need. Most people will achieve their peak performances when they are experiencing the thrill and satisfaction of doing a task well. When you add in the anxiety of worrying about consequences, performances typically drop. Of course there are those individuals, such as professional athletes, who perform their best under pressure. But that is the exception and not the rule. When you are able to lessen your self-demands and to learn not to be your own toughest critic (which you will learn more about in chapter 7), you will find yourself able more often to keep your arousal at optimal levels and to achieve your best.

CHAPTER 6

COPING WITH THE BLUES

Some Thoughts about the Blues

Almost everyone experiences periods of time characterized by listlessness, lowered enthusiasm for life, the blues, loss of humor, and feelings of being less than fully competent. For many persons these periods may last for hours or days, or a week at the longest. Some can turn to other persons, to tasks, or to leisure time activities to restore their feelings of competence and well-being. However, for others, these feelings lead to a long period of lower than normal productivity. The low productivity can lead to negative thoughts about oneself, which can serve to deepen the depression, thereby leading to lower productivity, et cetera. There are many different ways to break out of this cycle. The ideas presented here are strategies for behaving and thinking.

We need to *distinguish the symptom of depression from the disorder* of depression. The *disorder* of depression is the type of depression that may perpetuate itself physiologically, and for which a person may, in some cases, need medication in addition to a talking form of therapy. When we use the term "the blues" we're talking about the *symptom* of depressed mood - a condition from which most of us suffer at some time in our lives. Depressed mood may be serious, but does not involve the physical changes that character-ize a depressive disorder.

There are a great many possible causes of any individual's depressed mood. I view it as the outcome of a number of things, including a person's genetics, nutrition, medical condition, personal habits; or a variety of social factors including family, work, recreation, and romance. An extensive discourse on depression is beyond the scope and purpose of this discussion, but I will describe a few typical causes of the blues.

One common cause of depressed mood is loss of a sense of per-sonal effectiveness. We all need to feel some sense of mastery in our lives. However, in our complicated world, achieving mastery is difficult. If a person's strengths and resources fall short of the demands of a situation, a depressed mood may result. If you con-sider all the different ways in which the world challenges us to be resourceful and in control, you can appreciate how common it is for people to lose that sense of mastery. While some people take setbacks and failures in stride, others fall victim to depressed mood.

A second typical cause of depressed mood is overbearing self-de-mands. We all suffer setbacks in our endeavors, but some people are more prone than others to become depressed by them. These are often persons who have unarticulated but rigid rules for them-selves. For instance, if a person has a rule that says:

> *"I should be competent, achieving, and in control all the time, and it is awful if I'm not,"*

that person is more likely to become depressed over a setback than a person who lives without the burden of that uncompro-mising rule.

Most people in our culture strive to be achieving. A more relaxed rule, which would still propel us toward success, would be:

"It is satisfying, rewarding, and preferable to be competent and achieving, so I will strive for it. And if I sometimes fail, it is disappointing, but it is not awful and I will get over it."

If this last statement were our personal rule, we might still be highly motivated to achieve, and we might even be more capable of our best effort. I will use work that I did with a client I will call Ben to make this point:

Ben was so wrapped up in trying to succeed at everything that he would tie himself up in knots over it. I asked Ben if he thought it was "necessary" for him to be competent and achieving at all times, and he said "absolutely." I told Ben that he was mistaken, and that while it may be advantageous for him to be competent, it was only his preference, and not necessary. The idea that preferences and necessities are different began to help him to suspend his self-defeating attitudes.

I asked Ben how much human beings are worth and whether there is anyone who can judge the worth of a human being. I did not ask if we can judge a person's abilities, but whether we can judge a person's totality or essence. Of course, he said "no." I stated that if his totality . . . his essence . . . his worth as a human being cannot be judged, then it is not at stake when he attempts a project. This point added to Ben's suspension of his self-defeating beliefs.

I finally convinced him. I asked if he had ever played organized sports - with official league standings, umpires, et cetera. He said that he had played many organized team sports. Then I asked if he had ever played sports in a completely relaxed setting, such as a summer picnic, in which there was no pressure to win. He had. I asked if he had ever noticed that he played his very best at the summer picnic game. That was it. The light went on for Ben. When he plays an organized sport like softball, he does pretty well, but he is always a little nervous and tight. He cannot seem to loosen up enough to make a really spectacular play. However, in a pick-up game at a picnic with friends, he really shines. It is as if all his ability is there for him to use, whereas in an organized game some of his ability is inhibited by nervousness.

It is an apparent paradox. We do our best when we are having a good time and do not pressure ourselves to do our best. This works not only in sports but in intellectual and professional situations as well. Ben was forced to change his point of view. Success is a preference. It is worth striving for, but it's not necessary.

What about being admired? You may wonder if people have rigid, uncompromising rules about that. They do indeed. A person may have the unconscious rule:

> *"I should and must be liked, admired, and respected by all the persons who are significant to me; and if I'm not, it is proof that I'm an undesirable.*

The reasonable, compromising rule would be:

> *"Since it is great to be admired, I'll try to be; but if I am not, it is just a disappointment and not the end of the world."*

Another cause of depressed mood is growing up feeling unloved in the family. If children feel loved most of the time -- not for doing anything special, but just for being themselves -- they tend to grow up to be adults who feel good about themselves, even when circumstances are difficult. Children who grow up feeling that they constantly have to earn their love and acceptance tend to grow up to be adults who suffer depression when things do not go well.

Once people have already grown up with the feeling that just being themselves is not enough to ensure being loved, what can they do about it? This is where psychotherapy may be appropriate. It is very difficult for a person to change this state of mind without some skilled help.

Some people worry that psychotherapy means years of analysis, but that is not often the case. The time required varies a very great deal, according to the theories and methods of the psychologist, the adeptness of the client at learning to use therapy, and the severity of the problem. In my experience, most individuals can do a lot of productive work in four to twenty sessions.

The Road to Recovery

I have identified some causes of depressed mood. What are the remedies? Although *my suggestions do not necessarily apply to any particular person or situation*, I will list some measures you may take to recover your energy and zest for life.

l. Don't fight the depression. Try to see it as an opportunity to get a little rest from your usual energy state.

2. Let yourself run on "slow," but avoid "stop." Whatever your normal list of activities or tasks look like, cut it down to a size you can handle in your lowered energy state. Unless it is impossible, do not completely abandon your usual activities or tasks.

3. Think about the persons and activities that typically make you feel good, smile, or laugh. Try to arrange visits with those persons or participation in those activities. If this does not work, **tell yourself that it will work again later**.

4. Avoid medicating yourself with alcohol. It will only deepen the depression.

5. At whatever level you can handle it, get some exercise. If this means going for a walk, go. If it means lying on the floor and doing stretching exercises, do them. Do not exceed your physical capabilities. Remember that you will probably not exercise as vigorously as when you are not depressed, but do exercise.

6. Don't forget: there is an out-of-doors. Even if you do not really feel like it, consider going outside. You may be glad you did.

7. Convince yourself that no human being can judge the worth of any other human being. Therefore, your worth cannot be judged. It is not at stake. Many things may be at stake, but your worth as a human being is **not** one of them. You may just as well accept the idea that you are worthy because you exist.

8. Try to get your personal habits stabilized. Do your best to eat healthy foods, and try to go to bed and to rise at regular times.

9. Figure out which people in your life criticize you the most and, if possible, **avoid them!**

10. Seek help and support from others. If you have friends, neighbors, and relatives who can help, let them. If not, or if you think you are overburdening them, seek professional help. It does not make you weak to seek help with your emotions any more than it

makes you weak to seek help with your car repair, medical illness, or your taxes.

It is easy for me to list suggestions, but I must emphasize that the suggestions do not necessarily apply to any particular person or situation. Each person is an individual, and your own particular situation may require some skilled help. If so, please do not deny yourself that advantage.

Getting out of a Slump

Mr. C, a school psychologist, enjoys a highly successful, busy, and organized career. He has one full-time job, one adjunct teaching position, and two consulting jobs. He organizes his professional tasks in detail, keeping files, calendars, and appointment books. He plans his tasks according to semesters, weeks, and days. He is usually energetic, but comfortable. He finds time to exercise and stay fit, and believes that the exercise contributes to his energy and alertness.

However, on occasion, at irregular intervals, averaging about twice a year, Mr. C. goes into a slump. He loses his usual energy, and feels anxious and overwhelmed by tasks that he usually accomplishes with relative ease. Every time Mr. C. goes into a slump, he wonders how he got there and when, if ever, he will regain his usual energy and feelings of competence. Mr. C. does not suffer from clinical symptoms of a major depression, such as sleep and appetite disturbances during these episodes; he just loses his motivation and energy.

Mr. C. has read Dr. Nathan Kline's book, From *Sad to Glad*, and he agrees with Dr. Kline's concept that occasional depression is evidence of a need for the human organism to restore itself due to the vast complexity of tasks of which it is capable. Unfortunately, this does not comfort Mr. C. during his depressed episodes. He continues to fight the depression - to look at his usual long lists of tasks, and to make negative statements about himself when a day ends with no accomplishments.

Finally, on the author's advice, Mr. C. decided to accept the depression - to "go with it" - and to set significantly lower expectations for himself when these episodes occur. In effect, he uses time-management in reverse order, scaling down to a few tasks per day. Mr. C. decided that when he feels he is in a slump he will be satisfied with the day's accomplishments if he writes one report and runs one mile. Although these tasks will be far below his normal day's achievement level, Mr. C. accepts this very small list of expectations as sufficient for a day during a slump. Mr. C. begins to feel less anxious during his occasional depressed episodes. Best of all, because he has accepted a lower set of expectations during these times, he makes far fewer negative statements about himself, and the depressed episodes, though still occurring, are shorter.

In essence, Mr. C. has changed an inner rule that formerly said, "You should be maximally productive all the time." The scaling down of the usual time management techniques was made possible by the dropping of this former directive, and it improved the quality of Mr. C.'s life.

The first task associated with creatively managing a slump is to recognize and label the experience. It is not important what you choose to call it - "slump," "endogenous depression," "the blues" - but it is important that you do recognize and put a name to the episode so that you can activate your depression-fighting plans or your slump contingency method.

Slumps tend to be self-perpetuating for persons for whom productivity is a high value. Since the slump lowers accomplishment, and feelings about self are likely to be influenced by achievement, a vicious cycle is easily started. It is very important that you be willing to accept - temporarily - a lower standard for your own productivity.

A short slump is not typically very disruptive of one's life. The longer the slump, the more likely it is to be damaging. The way to interrupt the vicious cycle of a slump and to restore feelings of well-being, energy, and motivation is to do away with the negative self-talk and self-criticism that is likely to accompany the lower productivity. This could be done by using an act of will to immediately snap out of it and by retaining normal energy levels. However, since a troublesome slump is by definition an experience of lower motivation and energy, such an act of will may not be possible.

It may be better for you to accept the fact that this is a slump and to set a markedly lower agenda for the day, but to set a small agenda nonetheless. If you are **not** willing to assign fewer tasks for yourself during these episodes, you run the risk of doing absolutely nothing. This is due to feelings of being overwhelmed by the thought of the usual, high set of expectations. The key then is to proceed in a steady, persistent manner toward achievement of the reduced daily agenda, and to pat yourself on the back at the end of the day for doing okay under the circumstances.

If you maintain high expectations and end up doing nothing, you will fall much further behind than you would fall if you accomplished a reduced set of tasks. The further behind you fall, the more discouraged you will be, and the more discouraged you feel, the longer the slump will last.

If you recognize and label the slump, set a smaller agenda, work steadily on the remaining tasks, and pat yourself on the back for doing well under the circumstances, you will find yourself falling only somewhat behind. You will recognize that you are not as far behind as you otherwise might have been, and will have good feelings about yourself for having adapted well to the condition. The more you recognize yourself as adaptive, the more confidence you will have. The more confidence you have, the more energy you feel. The more energy you feel, the sooner you will be living and working with your usual motivation and verve.

Do not try to kid yourself! You really **do** have to accept a period of lower productivity in order for this method to work. Once you have successfully tried this method, you will find that your slumps occur less frequently and are of shorter duration. You may even welcome an occasional slump, knowing that it will not last long, will not put you far behind, and that it may provide a needed respite.

CHAPTER 7

PRACTICE RATIONAL THINKING AND YOUR LIFE WILL BE EASIER

Thoughts give rise to feelings. This simple fact is of great importance for us in terms both of self-understanding and self-improvement. One of the basic irrationalities common to many humans, as identified by Albert Ellis, is "It is **necessary** for me to be competent and achieving in all situations, and it is terrible and awful if I am not." If we still hold this belief, then Self improvement will **not** be a series of enjoyable techniques that make life more delightful. Rather, they will be a series of necessary-but-oppressive techniques needed to avoid the disaster of less than full competence.

It is vital that you truly appreciate the distinction between a necessity and a preference. You may prefer to be liked, admired, respected, competent, and achieving. However, none of these are **necessary**. As Dr. Ellis was fond of asking, "Where in the universe is it written that you **should** or **must** be competent?!" Self improvement techniques are best treated as a means to achieve a desirable, preferred end of your choice, but not as a means necessary to avoid disaster.

Learn to recognize and eliminate imperatives from your vocabulary (words such as "should, must, ought, and have to"). The moment you think that events **should** be different from the way they are, you are setting up an irreconcilable difference that can only result in loss of happiness. Although you may **prefer** to be more organized and productive in the future, and may decide to learn techniques to achieve that goal, you may as well **accept yourself exactly as you are right now**.

Learn to make the rational process part of your everyday thinking. Strive to be as competent as possible, and to influence events to turn out as favorably as they can. But, you may as well accept yourself exactly as you are, because that is exactly how you are. And, you may as well accept events exactly as they turn out, because that is the way they turn out.

As Murphy's infamous law predicts, "If anything can go wrong, it will." Since you are human, you **will** make mistakes and be less than perfect. To demand perfection of yourself or of events is to decide **in advance** to be frustrated and unhappy. Making these new thinking patterns your own many not spare you feelings of frustration, disappointment, and sadness when appropriate. However, rational thinking can very easily help you face adversity feeling **merely** frustrated or disappointed, and not severely upset and anguished.

Overcoming Self-defeating Thoughts

1. How many times have you said "I can't stand it"? 500 times? 1,000 times? 150,000 times? Every single time you were incorrect; you "stood it" every time. However, saying it made you feel worse. Get in the habit of **not** saying it.

2. Have you ever said, "I am my own worst critic"? (Most people do feel this way). You are probably much more critical of yourself

than you would be of someone else who performs as you perform. You would be better off convincing yourself that your double standard is irrational. You are assuming that there are two types of human beings in the world: 1) you, and 2) the rest of the world; and that **one set** of standards applies to the rest of the world and another **special set** applies to **you**. That is pretty arrogant, is it not? Try giving yourself the same leeway you give others. It is only fair.

Rational Coping Thoughts

1. You cannot judge the worth of any human being. You can judge a person's attributes - his or her talents, etc. - but you cannot judge the essence, or the worth, of any person. It follows that you cannot judge your own worth. Therefore, you cannot rationally say that your own worth depends on your accomplishments. If you are feeling anxious about your performance at any upcoming event, say to yourself "I want to do well, and I will put forth my best effort, but my worth as a person is **not** at stake."

2. When you are anxious about whether events will turn out in your favor, be sure to distinguish appropriately between what is preferable and what is necessary. Food, water, air, sleep, and elimination are necessary for life to continue. Academic achievement, professional status, esteem, material success, love, and athletic prowess may be preferable, but they are **not** necessary. No, they are **not**! You may want them very much, but they are **not** necessary for your survival. They are merely preferable. Convince yourself of this fact. It will help you to strive for your preferences in a less anxious and more effective manner.

3. When people are presented with inconvenient, painful, or unfair situations, they often say, **"It should not be this way,"** or

thoughts to that effect. In a way, this is an attempt to wish away what is real. It is a refusal to accept reality. There is a new and popular expression: "It is what it is." Although we may already have become tired of hearing the idea expressed with these particular words, there is nonetheless some wisdom in them. If we can teach ourselves to stop insisting, "things should not be this way," it will help us to remain more calm and healthy in the face of inconvenience and misfortune.

Section III
Managing Stress and Strain

The definitions from physics for stress and strain will help us to clarify our experiences and our coping methods. In physics, stress refers to a force applied to an object, and strain refers to the rearrangement of molecules within the object in response to the stress. In human terms, stress refers to forces the environment imposes on us, and strain refers to our biological and emotional responses to those forces. The word "stressor" is often used to emphasize the idea that stress is force acting on us.

The following are all examples of stress: the expectations of your family, tasks expected of you at work, traffic on the road, bills to be paid, newscasts on radio or television, an event to attend, the sound of a siren on the road, and even the words that you are reading on this page. Any stimulus that, as an organism, you have to react to constitutes stress. A simple way to put it: stress equals stimulation.

One immediate implication of this definition is that stress is not necessarily bad. After all, without stimulation we would not be able to thrive. To manage stress is **not** to eliminate all stimulation, but rather to exert some control over the amount and types of stressors to which we are subjected and to manage the intensity of our reaction.

Strain in human beings takes many forms. Included are physical tension, emotional anxiety, depression, procrastination, burnout on tasks and obligations, disruption of personal habits, sleep disturbance, alcohol abuse, self-criticism, and loss of pleasure in pastimes. The questionnaire entitled "Being Specific about your Experience of Stress and Strain," shown in Chapter 8, will give readers a chance to assess their experience of stress and strain in FIVE major categories.

Since it would be awkward to continually use the words "stress and strain," and even to switch back and forth between them, I may lapse into just using the word "stress." But seeing these as two separate phenomena - environmental forces and your responses to them - will help you to understand your experiences and manage your coping strategies.

CHAPTER 8

YOUR EXPERIENCE OF STRESS AND STRAIN

Stress has multiple causes, and strain is felt in many different ways. To learn more about these factors in your daily life, check **all** those items below that are typically true of you or that have been true of you recently.

SITUATIONS / OBLIGATIONS

_____I keep thinking about tasks I have not done.

_____I have so many things to do that I cannot concentrate on any one task without being distracted by thoughts about another.

_____I know I should write to relatives and friends, and I worry that they feel neglected.

_____I have some material possession, such as a car, home, stereo, or computer that I worry about because I know it needs maintenance.

_____Sometimes I fall behind on my many obligations.

_____I sometimes become irritated while searching for some document or form that I've misplaced.

_____I have places in my home, car or desk that are a cluttered mess, but I can't seem to get going and correct the situation.

HABITS

_____I often feel tired or tense due to insufficient Sleep.

_____I sometimes get jittery from drinking coffee.

_____If I exercised more often, I think I would be able to relax better.

_____I sometimes eat pastries or chips instead of a meal.

_____Sometimes I overdo it a little when I use alcohol to unwind.

_____I often skip breakfast.

_____I make no particular effort to keep regular sleeping hours.

_____On week-ends I try to make up for the sleep I miss during the week.

_____I know I should exercise, but it is so unpleasant and arduous.

THOUGHTS

_____It is necessary for me to be competent and achieving.

_____I should have respect and approval from all persons important to me.

_____If I am waiting for something important, I do not let myself think about anything else.

_____When things go poorly for me, I often say, "I can't stand it."

_____I have to keep the pressure on myself so I will be motivated to do well.

_____I am my own worst critic.

_____People should behave better than they do.

PHYSICAL TENSION

_____I can feel my stomach tying itself in knots.

_____I feel jittery enough that my hands shake.

_____I get headaches when I am under a lot of stress.

_____Sometimes my neck and shoulders get stiff or sore from feeling tense.

_____I have found myself engaging in nervous "tics" or mannerisms.

_____My shoulders or neck become tired from driving a car.

_____When I do relax, I realize just how tense I have been.

_____My jaw sometimes feels tense or clenched.

RECREATION

_____I almost always play to win.

_____I get disappointed when I lose a game.

_____I do not let myself just relax and enjoy myself when there is work to be done.

_____In a movie, or with friends, my mind drifts to my obligations.

_____It has been a long while since I have had a really relaxing vacation.

_____I rarely listen closely to music because I am thinking so much.

_____I just do not "kick back and relax" the way I used to do.

The areas in which you have made check marks may be areas that warrant your attention. Chapters 9 through 12 will provide you with information and strategies to help you deal more effectively with stress. You may want to refer back to the stimulus questionnaire now and then as you read the following chapters.

There are many ways of dealing with stress. Chapter 9 will provide an overview of both constructive and destructive ways.

CONSTRUCTIVE AND DESTRUCTIVE WAYS OF DEALING WITH STRESS AND STRAIN

Remember our simple definition of stress: stress equals stimulation. Stress is normal, and it is normal for us to sometimes experience strain in the form of emotional anxiety or physical tension. We all have these experiences at times, in a number of ways, such as emotional anxiety, irrational thinking, disrupted habits, physical tension, and loss of pleasure. In most cases, strain can be reduced and managed through constructive ways of thinking and behaving. However, individuals often cope with strain in unhealthy ways.

Destructive Ways of Dealing with Stress

-- Excessive escapist activity (e.g., television, movies, parties) to try to avoid facing tasks, feelings, or issues.

-- Drug and alcohol abuse.

-- Overeating or under eating

-- Withdrawal from family, work, or social contacts.

-- Dependence on a simplistic philosophy or religious cult to try to   remove feelings of responsibility for oneself.

These means of dealing with stress are considered to be destructive **if** they are excessive, **if** they are intrusive on others, **if** they fail to help you to attain positive health and well-being, or **if** they are your **only way** of coping. In other words, it is **not necessarily destructive** if, after a hard week at school or work, you go to a party and drink alcohol.

However if, in order to unwind, you play your stereo so loudly and with the bass turned up so high that you intrude on your neighbors, that is destructive. If your usual routine is to get up at 9:00 a.m. Saturday and go jogging, but you are too hung over from Friday night's drinking to do so, there is something destructive about that. If you drink to the point of intoxication and then drive your car, it is potentially extremely intrusive on others, and it is destructive. If you must party and drink every Friday night because you have no other methods to relax and unwind, that is destructive. I hope that these comments communicate that there is a great deal of leeway in healthy, constructive reactions to stress.

Constructive Ways of Dealing with Stress

1.   We can analyze our roles, tasks, and expectations in life. We can consider whether it would help us to improve our skills. We may either learn more efficient ways of meeting expectations, or find ways of reducing the expectations placed upon us.

2.   We can analyze our habits regarding eating, sleeping, exercise, and substance use. We can experiment with changing certain

habits to find out if a change would help us to deal more effectively with the strain of disrupted habits.

3.   We can practice thoughts that maintain our motivation but that lessen the strain of anxiety. There are certain ways of thinking that heighten strain. For instance, we increase strain by telling ourselves we "should or must" be perfectly competent, or that we "should or must" be admired by everyone. The rational thought that competence and popularity are desirable but not necessary can help us immeasurably.

4.   We can learn a simple, systematic method for relaxing ourselves, using a set of non-strenuous physical exercises. We may learn to use imagery as a shortcut to the same deep relaxation that we can achieve with the exercises.

5.   We can assess our recreational pursuits, and their effect on the strain of loss of pleasure. In particular, we may look at the issue of whether we "play" - that is, whether we have any activity in which our primary, genuine purpose is enjoyment and in which we do not have performance standards for ourselves.

You will notice that the five constructive means of dealing with stress and strain coincide with the 5 sections on the stimulus questionnaire. The five constructive methods just mentioned have just been described in the most brief and general terms. Method number 1, strategic means of dealing with stress, will not be elaborated upon now. The reason is that much of this book is devoted to strategic means of dealing with stress, by enhancing the effectiveness and efficiency of our lifestyle and work style in a number of ways. Method 3 was discussed in Chapter 3, "Think Rationally and Your Life Will Be Easier," and methods 2, 4, and 5 are the topics of the next three chapters.

CHAPTER 10

YOUR PERSONAL HABITS

In this section, we concern ourselves with the personal habits that influence our ability to manage stress.

Nutrition

You may wish to develop nutritional habits that are appropriate to your tastes, the demands of your lifestyle and, in some instances, the tenets of a philosophy. The following are a few nutritional measures that may be helpful:

1. *Use salt in moderation.* Check food labels for sodium in any of its forms, and use foods containing sodium sparingly. Although sodium is necessary for survival, excess salt is sometimes implicated in high blood pressure.

2. *Use refined sugar sparingly.*

3. *Get into the habit of eating breakfast.* Be sure to have some food containing protein at breakfast.

4. If snacking is part of your eating pattern, *choose foods such as fresh or dried fruit, low-fat cheese, nuts, or yogurt* instead of the typically high-fat foods commonly known as "junk food."

5. *Learn about the nutritional requirements that human beings have for protein, vitamins, and minerals.* Be sure to satisfy the recommended daily allowances, especially for the B-vitamins.

6. *Avoid "dieting" to lose weight.* Weight loss diets eventually fail, because the dieter eventually goes back to "regular eating." The only way to lose weight and to keep it off is to establish "regular eating patterns" that suit your body's needs, and to engage in regular exercise.

7. *Learn about the fat content of foods, and control your intake of fat.* Fat is a necessary for many of your body's functions, including the maintenance of cell walls. But excess fat is unhealthy. It is often recommended that we limit fat to thirty percent of our total calorie intake. Some of the recommendations often made include substituting fish or poultry for beef, eating more fruits, vegetables and grains, and avoiding fried foods.

8. *Foods such as whole grain breads and cereals, beans, nuts, fruits, and vegetables contain fiber.* A diet high in fiber is good for colon health, and prevents constipation. There is mounting evidence that a high fiber, low fat diet can help to control weight, reduce the likelihood of heart disease, and prevent colon cancer.

9. *Enjoy your coffee - in moderation* . It is still uncertain whether coffee is a contributing cause of such problems as cancer, high blood pressure, and heart disease. If you drink more than two cups per day, then perhaps it would be prudent to reduce that intake. Otherwise, enjoy your moderate coffee intake and concentrate instead on getting sufficient exercise and on eating a low fat, high fiber diet.

10. *Drink plenty of water* - perhaps six to eight glasses per day. As we age, we may experience less thirst, but the need to replenish fluids is still there.

11. *Wait before going for "seconds."* It usually takes a while for the feeling of fullness to set in.

12. *Avoid eating while watching television, talking on the phone, reading to your child, studying, or listening to music.* Those activities may take your attention away from the eating. If you have a need for a certain amount of pleasure from eating, you may find yourself overeating to attain it because you have "wasted" the experience of eating while distracted by other stimulation.

13. *For the most part, eat the foods you want.* In moderation, almost any food can be fit into a healthy eating regimen. If you have occasional strong cravings for a food that you know is unhealthy due to being high in fat or sodium, only eat it now and then. It will typically do you no good to try to resist a strong craving for a favorite food all the time. However, to make your overall eating plan a healthy one, it will probably be advisable for you to compensate by more strictly avoiding unhealthy foods that you do not really crave. For instance, if you sometimes have strong cravings for oatmeal cookies, perhaps you need to allow yourself this treat now and then. However, if you do not experience strong cravings for pie or cake, avoid them. By avoiding pie and cake, perhaps you will have left room in your overall eating regimen for occasional oatmeal cookies.

14. Assuming that you are not lactose intolerant, *drink milk or eat yogurt, cottage cheese, or low-fat cheese.* These foods contain the important mineral calcium. If you take calcium in a pill supplement, take it between meals so that it will not interfere with your body's absorption of iron.

15. *Consult a professional nutritionist if you have any question about your eating habits and their effects on your health.*

Exercise

You are probably aware of the types of exercises that work best for you with regard to your lifestyle, tastes, and physical limitations. Exercises that require your lungs to oxygenate blood continuously, and that require your heart to pump that blood continuously to your extremities, are known as cardiovascular exercises. Jogging, swimming, bicycling, vigorous dancing and brisk walking are all activities that exercise your cardiovascular system. So are such continuous action sports such as volleyball, racquetball, and tennis if, in fact, you keep moving. These exercises can help you, both physically and emotionally, to reduce the effects of stress and reduce tension and anxiety. Chapter 26 will be devoted to helping you to learn how to adhere to a fitness regimen.

Substances

Caffeine and **nicotine** are both stimulants, and have, among their various effects on the body, the ability to quicken heart rate and elevate blood pressure. Although many users profess to be "calmed down" by these substances, their physiological effect is one of arousal, and not of sedation. **Alcohol** is another substance often used by persons as a stress reducer. Alcohol does indeed have a sedating effect, and can create a sensation of calm by cutting down your ability to perceive stimulation coming in from your body's periphery. However, this effect can produce illusions. For instance, many persons bring a substance such as brandy with them in cold weather as a means of warming up. And indeed, a few nips of brandy in cold weather will give the user a feeling of warmth. However, the feeling is an illusion caused by diminishing signals from the nerve endings in the periphery. In actuality, alcohol makes us colder by dilating the blood vessels in the extremities, allowing more blood to migrate to the parts of the body that most efficiently radiate away our body heat.

Another problem can occur for some persons who may use alcohol as a sedative to induce sleep. Although alcohol can produce drowsiness, it can disturb sleep and cause frequent awakenings. It is probably in your best interest to carefully monitor your use of these and other substances, and to evaluate their effects on you. You will then be in a better position to decide whether your use of substances would best be left as it is, moderated, or discontinued.

Sleep

Your pattern of wakefulness and sleep and your experience of stress/tension/anxiety influence one another. You may wish to work on your sleep habits. This could involve a decision to keep more regular hours, or it could require a more concerted effort to combat insomnia via a number of strategies.

Trouble falling asleep, sometimes known as "initial insomnia," is a rather common problem. You would have to speak with a psychologist or another helping professional one-on-one to know which of my comments would apply to you as an individual, but I will suggest a number of methods among which you may choose. The strategies that follow are organized into four categories:

A. your overall self-maintenance;
B. your patterns of waking and sleeping;
C. a bedtime ritual; and
D. what to do when you do not fall asleep.

A. Overall Self-maintenance:
1. Set aside a specific time and place each day to plan a schedule for taking care of your tasks and obligations.

This may help to control the anxiety that can contribute to the problem.

2. Learn a technique for physical relaxation, and practice it regularly.

3. Choose an exercise program that is consistent with your tastes, lifestyle, and physical condition, and exercise regularly.

4. Avoid the overuse of stimulants such as coffee, colas, and cigarettes.

B. Your Overall Patterns of Waking and Sleep:

1. Establish the same rising time every morning. Do not vary this by more than an hour or two on week-ends. This will help your body to establish a rhythmic pattern of sleep and waking.

2. Avoid taking daytime naps. Naps can diminish your need for nighttime sleep, and can reinforce an irregular sleep pattern.

3. Don't use your bed for watching T.V., studying, or worry. Reserve your bed for sleep so that you will have a strong association between your bed and sleep.

C. Bedtime Ritual:

1. Lie down to sleep only when you feel sleepy.

2. Use the last 15-30 minutes before bed for a bedtime ritual. Use such activities as showering, putting on night clothes, brushing teeth, stretching exercises, listening to a favorite, soothing musical piece, or reading. However, if you choose reading as a before bed activity, be sure to read something that is not suspenseful, and that does not concern your work, finances or commerce. This would be a good time to read about the natural world – topics that are fascinating but unrelated to day-to-day affairs.

3. Avoid stimulants for the 3 or 4 hours preceding bed-time.

4. Avoid heavy meals before bed. A glass of milk or a slice of cheese (foods containing calcium) may be helpful.

5. When you go to bed, assume a comfortable position, and tell yourself there is nothing you can do about your obligations until tomorrow. Think about what drowsiness, heaviness, and sleepiness feel like. Let those feelings creep into your body, and enjoy them. Keep your eyes closed and avoid looking at the clock.

<u>D. What to do when you do not fall asleep</u>:

1. When you realize you are not falling asleep, focus your mind on something other than self-defeating thoughts such as "It's happening again" or "I'll never sleep." Try to take a matter-of-fact attitude. Tell yourself that as long as you lie comfortably with your eyes closed, you **are** allowing your eyes and body to rest.

2. If sleeplessness continues or if restlessness ensues, rise, go to another room, and occupy yourself with a boring or monotonous task. Return to bed later when you are sleepy.

3. If monotonous tasks do not help you to become sleepy, and if you cannot get tomorrow's obligations out of your mind, then make a list of those obligations. Write down the next, small step you can take toward each obligation, and *write down the next time you can appropriately take that step.* Then, tell yourself that you will take that step at the appropriate time, and that right now your best preparation for your obligations is to rest.

4. When you return to bed, be sure to lie in a comfortable position, and to occupy yourself with an awareness of what drowsiness feels like.

A note about medication and alcohol:
Medication for sleep is probably not needed, and may be habit-forming. Sometimes, however, a persistent bout of insomnia may best be interrupted with medication. Once you have re-established rest and sleep, the anxiety surrounding the insomnia may be gone and you can proceed without the medication. If you do feel that sleepless nights are becoming a problem, first consult a psychologist to see what you can accomplish with your inner resources. If the sleeplessness persists, you may want to consult a physician and agree on a strategic use of medicine. Take the view that medicine is a short-term strategy.

As for alcohol . . . . . alcohol has a well-known sedating effect, and it can make you drowsy. However, alcohol also has an alerting effect, which is less pronounced but lasts longer. Thus, alcohol may help you drop off to sleep initially, but can lead to disturbed sleep and frequent awakenings.

A final note: If you are having difficulty sleeping, seek some help. You need your sleep.

CHAPTER 11

PHYSICAL RELAXATION

It really is biological, you know !

Since relaxation and anxiety are incompatible states of being, you can reduce anxiety by learning **and practicing** a method for experiencing deep physical relaxation. There is a set of non-strenuous physical exercises that work for an overwhelming majority of people. The exercises are known as "progressive muscle relaxation," and you can probably teach them to yourself after carefully reading the description that follows.

As far as the western world is concerned, progressive relaxation dates back to the early part of last century, when a physiologist named Edmund Jacobson devised them. Jacobson worked at Harvard University, Cornell University, the University of Chicago, and Bell Laboratories. He was a researcher who was interested in discovering what happens physically when people say they are tense, nervous, or upset.

What Jacobson and later researchers have learned is that when we feel nervous, there is a constellation of physiological changes. Our heart beats faster. Our blood pressure becomes elevated.

Our breathing becomes quicker. We sweat more. We secrete more adrenalin-related substances into the bloodstream, and we secrete more stomach acids. Our muscle fibers become shorter. There is an increase in the electrochemical energy in the nervous tissue that serves the muscles in the periphery of our bodies. And, T-lymphocyte cells, needed to fight infection, and also needed to recruit B-cells to further fight infection, are less active and less available when we are tense. They are especially less active if we are also depressed, without a means to alleviate the depression. Every major system of our bodies is affected ny physical tension . . . the muscular-skeletal system, the digestive system, the nervous system, the endocrine system, the circulatory system, the immune system and the skin.

Jacobson was looking for one of these physiological changes that could come under some voluntary control, so he chose the shortening of muscle fibers. If I were to write in this book that you can begin to relax by lowering your blood pressure ten points on both the diastolic and systolic measures, you would only be confused, laugh, or wonder why you purchased the book. But if I write that you can make your hand into a fist . . . feel the tension . . . and release it . . . this you can do. When you tighten up your muscles, you cause the muscle fibers to become shorter. If you release them, they can lengthen out again. If you let go of the tension all at once rather than gradually, the muscle fibers can lengthen out with some momentum, and can become longer and more relaxed than they were before.

There is a difference between actual physical relaxation and the subjective feeling of being relaxed. Physical relaxation is an event that can be measured by changes in such body functions as pulse, blood pressure, and the electrical activity in the nerves that serve the muscles. Subjective relaxation is simply the feeling or belief that we are relaxed. After working on a number of muscle groups, you will begin to feel subjectively more relaxed, and physiological changes will begin to take place in your body so that your relaxation will be a physical event as well as a subjective event.

The Progressive Relaxation Exercise

Read the following directions carefully. Once you have learned the sequence of the exercises, you may want to practice them once or twice a day for a few weeks. A trained psychologist can help you learn the exercises if you are not able to teach them to yourself.

1. Set aside a 15 minute period of time, and try to ensure that you will be left undisturbed.

2. Sit comfortably in an arm chair, or recline on pillows. Ensure that your back and neck are comfortably aligned.

3. Learn the difference between feelings of tension and feelings of relaxation. Do this by first tensing and then relaxing muscle groups as described in the following instructions. **Introduce only as much tension as you need to distinguish between feelings of tension and feelings of relaxation.** After two or three muscle groups, you will know the right amount of tension for you to introduce. Apply this procedure to your hands, arms, shoulders, forehead, eyes, tongue, jaw, buttocks, legs, and abdomen. Here are some specific instructions for doing so:

Start with your right hand. Make your right hand into a fist. Do not use all your strength - just a moderate amount of tension. Take a deep breath and hold it. And, exhale and let go. After a moment, stretch the fingers of your right hand out wide, and relax the hand, letting the fingers fall into a natural, relaxed position. Pay careful attention to the difference between tensed and relaxed feelings. Take a moment to appreciate this difference. Take a slow, deep breath, and exhale and relax. Next, make your right hand into a fist and straighten out your right arm. Make your right arm rigid and feel the tension right up to your shoulder. Take a deep breath and hold it. And, exhale and let go. Again, stretch the fingers of the right hand out wide, and let them fall into a natural, relaxed position. Again, notice the difference between the tight, tensed feelings and the relaxed feelings. Allow yourself to relax more with every breath you exhale. For the last time, make your right hand into a fist and straighten out your right arm, making your right arm rigid. Take a deep breath and hold it. And, exhale and let go. Stretch the fingers, and let them relax. Use your imagination. Imagine that the tension is draining down your right arm - through the elbow, forearm, and wrist - and out through your fingertips. Now let go and relax a little more. You will be surprised, and pleased, at how deeply you can relax.

Already you have learned a great deal about how much tension you have to introduce in order for you to fully appreciate and enjoy the feeling of relaxation. With this learning in mind, continue with your left hand and arm. After you have done the exercises with the left hand and arm just as with the right, proceed with your shoulders. Draw your shoulders up as though shrugging them. Take a deep breath and hold it. And, exhale and let go. Allow your shoulders to sink down as deeply as they want to go. Take a slow, deep breath. And, exhale and let go. Allow yourself to relax a little more with every breath you exhale.

Next, proceed to the muscle groups in your face and in your head. In this area, in particular, do not introduce a lot of tension - just enough so that you will appreciate and enjoy the difference between tension and relaxation. Start with your forehead. Wrinkle your forehead by gently knitting your eyebrows, and let go. After a pause, introduce some tension in your forehead by raising your eyebrows, and let go. Pay attention to what it feels like as the tension that you have introduced into this area fades away. Take a slow, deep breath. And, exhale and let go. Next, close your eyes. Then, close them just a little bit tighter - and, let go. This would be a good time to allow your eyes to remain closed, and to allow your eyes and your eyelids to feel comfortable, heavy and relaxed. Next, press your tongue against the roof of your mouth. And, let go. Pause. Now, place your teeth together in a good, firm, comfortable bite. Slowly and·gradually bite down harder, until you can feel the tension in your jaw, and then, let go and relax. Then, as though you were very sleepy and had to yawn, open your mouth very wide, just as though you were yawning. And, let go and relax. Notice what it feels like as the tension that you have introduced into your face and jaw gradually fades away and is replaced by feelings of relaxation. Again, take a slow, deep breath . . . and, exhale and relax. Allow total relaxation throughout your forehead and eyes, your face and jaw, your neck and shoulders, and your arms and hands.

Now, straighten out your right leg, bringing the heel off the floor. Draw your toes back toward your head, gently stretching the muscles in the calf. And, let go and relax. Gently draw your right leg back so your right foot can rest flat on the floor. Be aware of the difference between the tense feelings and the relaxed feelings. Repeat this procedure for your left leg. Take a slow, deep breath. And, exhale and relax.

The last muscle group that you will introduce any tension into will be the abdomen. Take a deep breath and tighten your abdomen. Hold this breath, and exhale and let go. Repeat this exercise. Then, focus your attention on your breathing, carefully noticing the way your abdomen feels as it gently rises and falls with each breath. Imagine tension leaving your body the way air might leave a deflating air mattress. Breathe fairly deeply but normally, and allow yourself to let go and relax even more with every breath you exhale.

Next, you will think about different parts of your body, and will give yourself permission to relax those parts even more, imagining that the muscles are becoming smooth and relaxed. Follow this procedure for the following muscle groups: forehead and eyes, face and jaw, neck and shoulders, arms and hands, upper body (including back, chest, and abdomen), and legs. As you imagine the muscles in these areas becoming smooth and relaxed, remember to give yourself permission to relax fully and deeply.

Imagine any remaining tension draining out of your muscles, leaving your muscles smooth and relaxed. Pause. Let your shoulders enjoy the feeling that they are sinking down as deeply as they want to go, leaving your hands and arms heavy and relaxed. Pause. Focus on a sense of letting go, leaving you with a sense of stillness, like a pond without a ripple. Pick one of the following three words: "peaceful, calm or serene."

Think that word to yourself as you exhale each of your next few breaths.

After you have become fully relaxed, and are ready to return to other activities, tell yourself that you will still feel very relaxed, but that you will also feel alert and refreshed.

Here is a summary of the progressive relaxation exercise:
1.   Set aside 15 minutes.
2.   Sit or recline comfortably, ensuring that your back and neck are comfortably aligned.
3.   Learn the difference between feelings of tension and relaxation. Do this by first tensing and then relaxing muscle groups as described in detail above.
4.   After first tensing and then releasing each muscle group, pay careful attention to the difference between tension and relaxation, and enjoy the relaxed feeling.
5.   Draw your attention to each muscle group again, one at a time. This time, introduce no tension; rather, just imagine the muscles becoming smooth and relaxed. Give yourself permission to relax fully and deeply.
6.   Breathe fairly deeply. Feel what your abdomen feels like as it rises and falls with each breath. As you exhale, say a word to yourself ("peaceful," "calm" or "serene").

Imagination: a Short Cut to Deep Relaxation

There are methods other than the progressive relaxation exercise with its "tense and release" procedures that can make you feel relaxed. In fact, other methods may result in a subjective feeling of relaxation as deep as with progressive relaxation. However, research by Gordon Paul, as well as my own dissertation research, suggests that the use of progressive relaxation results in deeper physical relaxation.

Short cut methods are very valuable when they are at first paired with progressive relaxation. Mental imagery is one such method. You can train yourself to become very deeply relaxed with progressive relaxation, and can subsequently learn to relax almost as deeply through the shorter method of imagery.

First you will have to construct for yourself a relaxation scene. This should be a scene in which you would feel particularly calm, comfortable, and relaxed if you were actually there. It may be a scene that you have actually experienced many times. For instance, it may be your favorite ocean beach, your favorite mountain trail, or your favorite chair in front of a fireplace. It could be a scene that you have experienced once or twice. For instance, perhaps you have a memory of being on a vacation and of floating down a river on a raft, or of sitting on a dock on a pond, and have a memory of feeling unusually peaceful. Alternatively, you could imagine a scene that you have never experienced, but that you believe may exist somewhere. For instance, you could imagine reclining and rocking on a hammock strung between two palm trees on a tiny paradise island in the South Pacific.

In order to create a powerful, useful scene, you will have to use your imagination to experience the SIGHTS, SOUNDS, FEELINGS, and AROMAS of your relaxation scene. I am going to describe a specific scene for you, using all of those methods of description. This will serve as an illustration for you so that you can then construct a scene of your own choice for yourself:

Imagine yourself walking barefooted down an ocean beach on a warm summer day. The sun is fairly high in the sky and behind you, and you can see your own shadow on the sand in front of you. Notice the way the sand looks when it is in direct sunlight compared to how it looks when covered by your shadow. The sky is a brilliant blue with a few fleecy, fluffy white clouds. The sunlight is sparkling off the surface of the water - silvery and shimmering. The ocean water is blue, and when the waves roll in you can see that blue water foam white. The sand, pebbles and stones on the beach are different shades of tan, grey, and white. See all you can see.

Imagine the sound of the waves rolling in on the beach. There is a deeper, more thunderous sound as the waves break, and a softer, hissing sound as they recede. The occasional call of a sea gull is a sharp, high-pitched sound. A half-mile out at sea there is a bell buoy, and you can hear the faint, distant sound of the bell ringing as the buoy rocks gently in the ocean swell. (That is the most distant sound you can hear). If you come to a pile of smooth, beach-polished pebbles and stones, and gently and idly kick them, you can hear the sound they make as they clatter together. (That is the nearest sound you can hear). Hear all you can hear.

Imagine the texture of the sand on your bare feet. Think about walking close to the water, where the sand has recently been covered. The sand there is firmly-packed and cool. If you walk on an angle away from the water, you will reach sand that has been left untouched by waves and tide. The sand there is loosely packed and very warm. The breeze is gentle and warm against your face. You can feel the warmth of the sun on your skin. Notice the feeling of being upright, on your feet, and of gently and rhythmically strolling along. Feel all you can feel.

Finally, there is the scent of the fresh, salty sea air, and any other pleasant aroma that you associate with an ocean beach.

Review in your mind's eye and your mind's senses the entire beach scene: blue sky … sunlight sparkling on the water … fleecy white clouds … colors of the beach … sunlight and shadow … the sound of the surf … the call of a sea gull … distant ringing of the bell buoy … nearby sound of pebbles clattering together … warmth of the Sun … breeze against your face … texture of the sand … rhythm of strolling … aroma of the fresh, salty sea air.

If you see anyone with you in your scene, imagine that that person is enjoying the tranquility of the scene just as you are, and that you do not have to relate to that person. There is no need to be concerned with doing or saying the right thing.

If there is anything at all in your scene that you experience as uncomfortable or distracting, remove it, even if doing so makes your scene unrealistic. And, if there is anything that you would like to add to your scene to make it even more comfortable, go ahead and add it - again, even if this means making the scene unrealistic.

Imagine that you have no obligations and no appointments. Give the scene a sense of endlessness.

After you have brought the scene vividly to mind and felt the sense of relaxation, say "so long" to your scene for the time being, remembering that you can return to your scene whenever you wish to in your mind's eye and with your mind's senses. Then think about your present environment and, when you are ready, open your eyes.

A Note about Sense Modalities

When describing the ocean beach scene, I used descriptive language in four senses: sight, hearing, touch, and olfaction. The first three were predominant. "Kinesthetic" refers both to the sense of touch and to the body's ability to detect body position and motion.

When you utilize mental imagery, you may find that you are not able to experience all senses with equal vividness. Do not let this worry you at all. It is typical for individuals to be able to imagine one or two senses clearly, and to be weak in at least one. If you find this to be true of you, do not struggle unduly to bring the weak sense into focus. You may improve your imagery in that sense mode in time, but the technique is quite useful without clarity in all senses.

Train Yourself to Use Imagery

As you begin to train yourself in deep relaxation, it will be especially helpful to use the tense/release exercises. For a week or two it will be beneficial to practice them twice a day. However, those exercises take ten to fifteen minutes to perform, and that is not always convenient. Furthermore, no matter how helpful you believe the exercises to be, in time they will lose out in competition with other obligations.

Therefore, it will be very beneficial to gradually discontinue the use of the tense/release exercises, and to rely on the following methods:

1. your memory of the feeling of being deeply relaxed.

2. focusing on muscle groups and imagining the muscles becoming smooth and relaxed.
3. deep breathing
4. thinking a word such as "calm," "peaceful," or "serene."
5. use of an imagined relaxation scene.

When you practice progressive relaxation, begin with the tense/release exercises, and then do the focusing method. Then, put yourself into your relaxation scene for a few moments - just long enough to deepen your relaxation somewhat. Then, end the exercise. There is no need to meditate on the relaxation scene. Just bring it to mind for a few moments.

Practice these exercises every day, preferably twice per day, using the relaxation scene at the end of the exercises. Make a list of all the muscle groups that you tense and release in the exercises. Place the name of the muscle group that is easiest for you to relax at the bottom of the list. Place the most difficult muscle group at the top. Once the exercises are working well for you, drop the tense/release exercise for the muscle group at the bottom of the list. Every two days, drop another muscle group.

After approximately two to three weeks, you will have abandoned the tense/release exercises completely. You will be relaxing effectively by A) remembering the relaxed feelings, B) focusing, C) breathing, D) saying a relaxing word to yourself, and E) using imagery. Congratulations! You have a set of natural, quick, unobtrusive skills at your disposal. Use these natural methods to relax at the earliest onset of tension in your daily life.

CHAPTER 12

RECREATION

In this category, we are considering those activities that provide respite from school, work, homemaking, or raising children, and that have the potential to ease your tension and anxiety. Here are a few ideas to keep in mind as you plan ways to minimize your responses to stress through recreational activities.

A. One key idea is respite - rest from the activities that are normally stressful to you. In order to provide relief from stress, a recreational pursuit may serve best if it is different from your work activities. Thus, for a newspaper editor, serious reading may not serve as well for recreation as a non-reading activity. For a taxicab driver, a "leisurely ride in the car" may not seem to be as restful as another activity would.

B. Not all recreation is "play" and you would do well not to confuse it as such. Here is my definition of play:

Play is an activity in which the primary purpose is enjoyment, and in which you set no performance standards for yourself.

According to this definition, if you engage in a game and end up disappointed if you do not win, you were not "playing" the game. If you do woodworking for recreation, but feel disappointed in yourself for not meeting a standard of excellence, then your woodworking is not "play." If you see a movie, and it matters to you whether you come up with a brilliant insight about the meaning of the movie or about the quality of the production, then for you, seeing a movie is not "play." These activities may take your mind off your usual work, and may therefore be recreational. But if you have performance standards for yourself and there is a chance for disappointment and frustration, the activity is not "play" - at least, not according to this one psychologist's definition.

It may be in your better interest to consider having at least one activity in your life in which you are satisfied with any level of performance - one activity in which you can do poorly and still find joy in the activity itself. All your recreational pursuits do not have to fit the definition of "play." You can experience rest from your responsibilities while involved in a recreational pursuit in which you do strive to attain a level of proficiency. But you are better off with at least one pastime that does fit the definition.

C. You may schedule recreation in many ways. You may store up your recreation needs for one long summer vacation. You may take a weekend off each month, or you may take ten-minute breaks four times a day. It is up to you to select the ways in which you can best refresh yourself and restore your energy.

Section IV
Time and Task Management

CHAPTER 13

MANAGE TIME AND TASKS WITH MODERATION !

Time management is not an all-or-none skill. We are not forced to choose between a highly managed, structured lifestyle and a totally unstructured way of being. It is not fun to be too structured, and it is not fun to be too disorganized! We may even effectively vary our use of time management and structure to suit various purposes and occasions.

In order to make this point as understandable, real, and emphatic as possible, examples will be given of the use of lifestyle management in moderation and on an "as needed" basis.

You Can Do It When You Really Want To

Mr. A, a medical technologist, likes to take part in many outdoor activities, such as mountaineering, white-water canoeing, and skiing. Mr. A can tolerate a certain amount of structure and detailed planning, but feels uncomfortable and "locked in" if he does too much of it. However, when Mr. A fails to plan ahead thoroughly, he finds himself at home many weekends due to a failure to arrange a canoe rental, failure to arrange in advance for a climbing partner, or any number of failures to attend to details. Mr. A finds no need to apply time management to his work, where his tasks seem to be completed according to routine, or according to casual adjustments made by mental notes but without extensive planning or list writing. Because he can handle his work life in a comfortable manner without additional detailed planning, Mr. A decides he can tolerate some detailed planning in order to improve his recreational life. He establishes a file box with names, addresses, and phone numbers of recreation areas, national parks, sporting goods dealers, outing clubs, and other outdoor enthusiasts. He begins planning week-end trips a month in advance, and establishes a list of equipment to buy, rent or repair; persons to contact, and licenses to acquire for each trip. Mr. A sets up certain times of the week to attend to those details, and reviews his task lists every evening. Although he started out disliking these detailed tasks, he soon finds that there are very few weekends in which he is not free to breathe mountain air or taste river spray. In short, he decides that a certain amount of detailed planning results in a worthwhile payoff of an enriched outdoor recreation life. Mr. A has applied time management selectively in his life. He still may not time manage household tasks, family obligations, or his work. He did apply time management for a specific purpose.

What if I only need organization some of the time ?
One of the ways in which we may set ourselves up to fail is to be inflexible in our style of task management. One possibility for us to consider is that we may alter our task management methods to meet the different requirements of different situations. The following story will illustrate this point.

Ms. B, a schoolteacher, finds herself listing, managing, and planning tasks more than she really prefers at her work. Therefore, she manages her personal, social, and recreational life without detailed planning. When it occurs to her to take care of a certain task, such as routine maintenance of her car, grocery shopping, or inviting friends to entertain, she does the task. She refuses to list, plan or otherwise manage these events. Ms. B usually feels comfortable with her lifestyle. However, twice a year she experiences considerable anxiety, and she loses confidence that she can complete all of the tasks that accumulate. These two times per year are Christmas and the end of summer, just before the start of the new school year. As Christmas approaches, Ms. B feels anxious about travel plans, Christmas card and gift lists, putting antifreeze into her car, and writing and correcting final examinations. As summer draws to a close, Ms. B feels overwhelmed by the necessity of getting her boat out of the water, doing some advance planning for classes, filling out her professional wardrobe, ensuring that her teaching contract is in order, and moving to a new apartment. Finally, Ms. B decides to continue to handle tasks and obligations in an unstructured way ten months of the year, but she decides that promptly on August 1 and December 1 she will make a detailed list of all she wants to complete. She specifies resources she will need to complete the tasks, and definite times she will set aside to complete them. She checks, amends, and re-writes her lists when needed.

Although she continues to feel somewhat oppressed by the apparent need to structure her life so strictly two months per year, she decides that she prefers this oppressed feeling to the anxious, overwhelmed feeling she formerly felt before applying time management. She still has 10 months per year to handle her non-professional matters in the unstructured fashion that she usually prefers. Ms. B has developed a cyclical use of time management techniques according to occasional need.

CHAPTER 14

HOW WE SET OURSELVES UP TO FAIL

This chapter contains three sections. The first will be a discussion of how you can limit yourself by allowing your past to exert too great an influence on your present. Then you will see how you can limit your success by limiting our imagination. Finally, we will discuss the strategic mistake of over-committing ourselves.

"I can't do it"

"Because something once strongly influenced my life,
it must go on controlling my feelings
and behavior today."

-- irrational belief identified by
Albert Ellis and Robert Harper

Think of your life as a meadow. Think of full enjoyment of life, with freedom of choice, as the ability to wander freely about the meadow. Now think of experiences that we refuse to consider, or opportunities that we refuse to entertain, as fenced-off areas where we cannot go. If enough parts of the meadow are fenced off, what remains can appear constricted and not appealing. Similarly, the years ahead of us in life can appear less appealing if we have already decided that many potential experiences from the "meadow of life" are to be avoided.

What makes us limit our lives in this fashion? Very often, it is unfortunate, uncomfortable, or even painful and traumatic experiences earlier in life. You have heard this type of experience and its results expressed numerous times.

- • • When I was little, my uncle threw me in the water and I was   terrified. Now I can never learn to swim.
- • • When I was sick in the hospital they fed me a lot of green beans. I cannot eat green beans anymore because they remind me of being   sick.
- • • When I was little, I used to be a big fan of the Texas A&M football team. I remember the University of Texas beating them solidly, so there is no way I will ever go to the University of Texas!
- • • I was ironing when I heard on the radio that Roosevelt died, and I have never ironed since.
- • • I was making love to my wife on 9/11/2001 when I heard about the terrorist attack on the twin towers, and I have never made love since then.

I threw in the last examples to show how truly ridiculous it is to think in this way. I hope there is no one for whom it is a true example. It is certainly understandable that we can develop an uncomfortable feeling associated with some food, event, location, or activity. We always have a right to our feelings. However, is it reasonable to allow ourselves to be controlled today by something that happened in the past?

If indeed we are still appear to be controlled by a prior experience, it is not actually that unfortunate experience that has us in its control. In reality, what limits us today is the belief that is printed at the start of this section. We are controlled not by past events themselves, but by our own belief that the past must go on controlling us today.

The Roman emperor Marcus Aurelius is credited with the following statement:

> *If thou are pained by any external thing, it is not this thing*
> *that disturbs thee, but thine own judgment about it.*
> *And it is in thy power to wipe out*
> *that judgment now.*

If you find yourself avoiding some type of activity or experience because of a past event, then it may be in your interest to identify the judgment or belief you hold today that is the actual reason you limit yourself. Then you may indeed have the power, as Marcus Aurelius said, to wipe out that judgment and to free yourself from a needless constriction of your life experience.

"I Can't Imagine Dong It"

Have you ever found yourself saying that you could not imagine doing something . . . something that might really be to your advantage if you would do it? I have heard it from scores - maybe hundreds - of individuals. Here are a few statements that I have heard:

- • • I can't imagine getting up in the morning and jogging.
- • • I can't imagine asking her/him out for a date
- • • I can't imagine applying for that type of Job.

• • • I can't imagine standing up for myself in that situation.
• • • I can't imagine writing a book.

I have a few stock answers when my clients say things like this. One of them is "Yet." In other words, I am telling them "You have *not yet* been able to imagine doing that." Another is "Try." ("Try to imagine doing it.")

There are clearly some tasks, feats, or adventures of which an individual is not capable. For instance, if I were to say, "I cannot high jump seven feet," it would not be helpful to reply to me, "You mean you cannot *yet* high jump seven feet." The fact is that no amount of attention to physical training, nutrition, and positive thinking will enable me to attain that feat.

But there are many things of which we are capable, but that we have never tried, never thought about - never imagined doing. In some cases, this may be no loss whatsoever. For example, I cannot imagine smoking a carton of cigarettes. In other cases, this may be a loss of an opportunity to push back our boundaries and to tackle something that could be rewarding. Just because we can imagine doing something, that is of course not a guarantee, or even an indication, that we can do it. However, if we *cannot* imagine doing something, then it is a sure bet we cannot do it.

Once we have identified something we would like to consider doing, but that we never done before, it is important for us to be able to imagine doing it. Many people use the word "visualization" for this process, but I prefer the word "imagery." Visualization clearly implies the sense of sight, whereas imagery implies use of all the senses in imagination. If we would like to consider doing something, it may help us to imagine ourselves - as vividly as we can - doing it. We can use our senses of sight, sound, touch, motion, and even aroma to make the imagery as vivid as possible.

This process can help us in a few ways. First, we may imagine some of the difficulties we would encounter, and can therefore think through solutions before the problem ever arises. Second, use of imagination may serve as a rehearsal. This is true even from the point of view of your body's nervous system. For instance, if you imagine ducking when you hear a loud noise, your nervous system will engage in some of the activity that is needed for you to actually duck. If you do not believe that the body reacts in preparation for stimuli not yet encountered, just think about what it would be like to bite into a lemon. Do you understand now?

The act of imagining doing something does not oblige you to do it. Even after deciding not to pursue a project you had imagined, you will feel as though you made that decision as a matter of choice and not due to a lack of capability. But if you do decide to pursue the project, you may find yourself better prepared to do so.

Let us illustrate this point by looking at the case of two construction workers, Cal and Lou. They were both intrigued with the idea of taking a summer off and backpacking through Australia and New Zealand. They had talked about it for years, but had made no moves whatsoever toward making the dream come true. They thought of it as "hot air ... a pipe dream."

Finally, they were instructed about how to set goals and take steps toward making them real. They first had to learn to imagine themselves doing such tasks as 1) going to the library and to travel agencies to read about Australia and New Zealand; 2) going to their local federal building and making application for passports;

3) saving money regularly to finance the trip; and 4) purchasing backpacks and experimenting with packing up enough light weight clothing and equipment to get by.

Once they had begun to imagine taking on these steps they were able to actually tackle them. For about a year, they took on the tasks, one by one. As the summer approached, Cal and Lou both requested and received leaves of absence for July and August. Cal had nothing to hold him back, and he made the trip. Lou, on the other hand, had finally decided to marry the woman he had been dating. He was torn between two alternatives: 1) making the Australia/New Zealand trip, and 2) using the money he had saved for building materials to start building a house for himself and his fiancée, and using the two months for building. He felt equally capable of either. Finally, he decided to stay and to invest his time and money for the house. Even though he had not made the trip, he reported in retrospect that he felt very good and capable, because by making preparations for the trip he had increased his confidence in his ability to make dreams into reality.

Over-Committing Ourselves

Putting too many tasks on our agenda is a common way to set ourselves up to fail. Here are two ways to combat this tendency. First, remind yourself often that life is a process more than it is a product. Life is a succession of "here and now" moments. Any one moment may feel enjoyable and rewarding, or rushed and unsatisfying. Most of us do indeed have many things we would like to accomplish, and productivity does have its advantages. However, if we put too many items on our agenda at one time, we will probably feel rushed and anxious. This is not the best frame of mind with which to excel. Moreover, we could prevent ourselves from enjoying the moment-to-moment experience of living.

Second, focus some attention on learning to make accurate predictions of how much time tasks will take. Most of us vastly underestimate the time it will take to accomplish a task. If you learn to overcome this tendency, you will be in a better position to avoid over committing yourself. If you need to actually write down your prediction of the time tasks will take, and later compare those predictions with the actual time, then do it. It will be worth whatever effort it takes for you to learn to make more accurate time predictions.

CHAPTER 15

TIME AND TASK MANAGEMENT BY INTERNAL REVIEW

Practically any new skill is meaningless until seen in the context of the individual's own personal style. When we have learned through experience what our own values and expectations are, we can make responsible and effective use of time management skills. Therefore, I have written the next exercise in the book not only to introduce some time management issues and techniques, but primarily to foster your exploration of your own priorities, attitudes and habits.

Management by Internal Review

You were told early in the book that you would be taught an internal monitoring technique relative to time management. I am going to describe an exercise that will allow you to try out such a technique. First, let your mind wander over the situations and events in your life concerning your material and financial life. Accept the fact that to this point you have done the best job you know how to do in relation to this aspect of your existence. If you become aware that there are some changes you would like to make in this area, think about the first, achievable step you would like to take toward the desired change. Identify clearly in your mind what your first concrete, achievable step will be. Then, just relax.

Now, turn your attention to those aspects of your life that relate to your physical condition and recreation. Once again, remember that you have done the best you know how to do thus far in your life. If there are any changes you would like to make in your physical and recreational life, think about the first, achievable step you would like to take toward the desired change. Identify clearly in your mind what your first concrete, achievable step will be. Again, just relax.

Next, turn your attention to the status of your social life. Think about your relationships with friends and family. If there is anything you would like to do to make this aspect of your life more satisfying, identify the first, achievable step you could take. When you have clearly identified that first achievable step, just relax again.

Now, turn your attention to the status of your home and domestic life. If there is anything you would like to do to make this aspect of your life more satisfying, identify the first, achievable step you could take. When you have clearly identified that first achievable step, just relax again.

Now turn your attention to your intellectual and spiritual life. Accept the fact that to this point you have done the best job you know how to do relative to this aspect of your existence. If you become aware that there are some changes you would like to make in this area, think about the first, achievable step you would like to take toward the desired change. Identify clearly in your mind what your first concrete, achievable step will be. Then, just relax.

Last, turn your attention to your professional or vocational life. Accept the fact that to this point you have done the best job you know how to do relative to this aspect of your existence. If you become aware that there are some changes you would like to make in this area, think about the first, achievable step you would like to take toward the desired change. Identify clearly in your mind what your first concrete, achievable step will be. Then, just relax.

You have now considered six aspects of your life:

1. material and financial
2. recreational and physical
3. social
4. home /domestic
5. intellectual and spiritual
6. professional / vocational

These six have **not** been arranged in order of importance. They were simply arranged so as to allow me to suggest the only memory device I could think of: "Mr. Ship."

M - Material
R - Recreational
S - Social
H - Home
I - Intellectual
P - Professional

You have planned at least one achievable task in each area that you could undertake to make that part of your life more rewarding. Remember that you have not signed a contract or in any other way obligated yourself. You have merely identified potential ways of working toward enhanced management of your life. You may work on one or more of these tasks. You may discard them all. You may set them aside for a while and consider them again later. You have increased your potential for more vital, purposeful living.

Use the memory device – "MR. SHIP" – to monitor these six important areas of your life experience. By internally monitoring these six categories, you will be able to reorder your priorities and/or manage your time without setting pencil to paper. In addition, this internal monitoring itself need not be scheduled, but you may wish to try this process whenever you feel anxious or unfulfilled. Edward's account may explain this latter point.

I'm not normally a nervous, anxious person. Once in a while, though, I would get this feeling . . . you have probably felt something like it. I would feel that I was forgetting something. I would feel nervous because I was sure there was something I should be taking care of that I was neglecting, but I just could not put my finger on it. It would just keep me nervous for quite a while, and in some instances, I never would really figure out what had caused the anxiety.

I was having one of these episodes one time while I was getting counseling from the author. He taught me his method of management by internal review, and when he came to the part about marriage and family life, it hit me. I was going to be the best man at my first cousin's wedding, and I did not know what was expected of me. I had not prepared any speeches. I had not bought any special gifts. I had been meaning to call to find out what was expected, but I had not done it yet, and that is what was weighing so heavily, though unconsciously, on my mind. As soon as I identified the problem, I decided I would call my cousin that very night, and the anxiety immediately lifted.

I use management by internal review now every time I have a feeling of anxiety that I cannot figure out. IIn most cases, I find that I can identify some obligation that I have forgotten to attend to. And, as soon as I make a

297 | 9781502995711 | 297

Location: BD-4

ZBM.YBTB

Title:	Your Life: An Owner's Guide: Goals, Dreams, Values, Exercise, Money and People
Cond:	Very Good
Date:	2023-08-24 10:11:49 (UTC)
mSKU:	ZBM.YBTB
unit_id:	11517887
Source:	CARMEN

delist unit# 11517887

XXXXX

plan to deal with the issue, the anxiety disappears. I love this method! It is so easy. It does not take calendars, lists, computers, or anything. I only need a few moments for an internal review.

The method of internal review may be used, as Edward employs it, as a response to a nagging feeling of anxiety about obligations unattended, or it may be used regularly as a means of time management not requiring lists or other tools. Either way, the method of internal review is a means that many readers may find to be very helpful in their efforts to manage their time and tasks effectively.

ORGANIZING TIME

How precious is your time ?

Twenty-two thousand days.
Twenty-two thousand days.
It's not a lot. It's all you've got.
Twenty-two thousand days.
Twenty-two thousand nights.
Twenty-two thousand nights.
It's all you know. So start the show.
And this time . . . . This time feel the flow . . . . . .
and get it right!
- - The Moody Blues

The Moody Blues are telling us that an individual's life is not forever. Twenty-two thousand days equals 60.27 years. That is shorter than the average life span in the western world. Nevertheless, it is probably about equal to the average life span starting from the age when a person may start listening to the Moody Blues, or reading self-help books.

How should we regard the time we have available to us? Should we make ourselves frequently aware of our mortality, and squeeze every experience and accomplishment we can into our days? Should we put our mortality, and any resulting sense of urgency, out of our minds and live in a more leisurely fashion, taking things as they come? Or is there some middle ground - some combination of the first two positions?

There is no universal right or wrong answer to these questions. There is not even an answer that is right for any individual all throughout his or her life. But, there are answers that may work for an individual at a period of time in his or her life.

What can you do with 5 minutes?

If you ever decide to keep a record of how you use your time during the course of a day, you will probably be impressed with the number of times you have a 2, 5, or 10 minute period of time that passes by with neither fun nor accomplishment. It may be helpful for you to identify the nature and variety of useful tasks or pleasurable interludes that can fit into short periods of time.

There are many uses of 5-minute blocks of time. You may choose to carry around stamped postcards, and to use five-minute intervals to write to friends and relatives with whom you might otherwise not correspond. If you are engaged in a writing project, you could carry a notebook or electronic device, and you could use five minutes to think of an idea and to jot down a few notes about it.

You may choose to use five-minute intervals to relax, meditate, or to reaffirm the joy of existence in other ways. For instance, I have sometimes used five minutes to try to identify all the different colors I could see, sounds I could hear, and physical sensations I could feel.

Whether you use them for fun or productivity, some of those short time periods that may now go wasted could be put to a better use.

The Inevitable Lists and Calendars

Time management habits may be seen to fall somewhere between the extremes of different variables:

rigid_____disorganized

persevering_____procrastinating

self-oppressive_____self-indulgent

achievement-oriented_____non-achievement oriented

1. Daily lists of tasks to accomplish are found by many individuals to be helpful. It is also helpful to have a routine time for preparation of a list, such as:
>   a. Last thing before retiring at night.
>   b. First thing in the morning.
>   c. First thing upon arriving at work.

Waiting until arriving at work is helpful for those persons who like relaxed and peaceful early morning preparations. Last thing before going to bed is helpful for those individuals who will not let go and sleep unless they feel they have a definite plan for the next day.

2. Tasks listed are best divided into achievable units. Listing a task that is so large or complex as to render it non-achievable in the day tends to lead to frustration.

3. Tasks on a list may be designated by priority signs, such as:

    a. I -   immediate.

    b. ST - short-term

    c. LT - long-term

4. Daily, weekly, or monthly lists may be written. Avoid too many lists that involve a great deal of cross-referencing among them.

5. After a task is completed, it may be helpful to draw a bold, visible check mark beside it. This may be done with a flourish, to remind us that we are organizing our lives to make life more delightful as well as more efficient. After three to five days, daily lists may be re-read, and items that have not received a check mark may be placed on a new list if they are still relevant.

6. It is advantageous for a person to be aware of his or her peak hours of efficiency, and to schedule difficult tasks requiring maximum concentration during those peak times.

7. It may be helpful to use a chart, with blocks for time periods, and to block out scheduled time. We can then see where our unscheduled time is, so that we can then work on our task lists.

8. If a certain amount of privacy is important to you, it may be helpful to block out private time. Remember that you have a need for a certain amount of private time and private space, and that if time management means no private time and space, time management may also mean self-oppression.

9. Be aware of the length and intensity of tasks. It may be important for you to intersperse lighter, shorter tasks among the heavier, longer tasks. In this way you will make more reasonable demands on your mental and emotional resources, and the act of accomplishing a few light, short tasks may buoy you up for the heavier, longer tasks.

CHAPTER 17

RELATING TO OTHERS

O ur ability to live effectively is always influenced by the human as well as the physical environment. On the positive side, other persons can advise us, encourage us, or even collaborate with us in our efforts. When relationships with others are characterized by understanding and consideration, those interactions put joy into our lives! On the negative side, other people can discourage or distract us. Just as interaction characterized by understanding and consideration can be one of life's primary joys, relationships characterized by misunderstanding and inconsideration can be one of life's major frustrations.

This chapter will consist of three sections. The first will be a brief selection of methods we can use to try to derive joy from considerate interaction with others. The second will be a discussion of the philosophy and a few of the techniques of assertive communication. The third will contain suggestions about relating to others when productivity and time management is at issue.

Encouraging Consideration

The words, "consideration" and "decorum" have similar meanings. However, I want to make what I believe to be an important distinction between concepts.

The American Heritage Dictionary defines *consideration* as "thoughtful concern for others." I want to be sure to distinguish this concept from that of decorum. *Decorum* has more to do with refinement. It implies "standards to be observed by one who makes a claim to good breeding." Thus, decorum is practiced in deference to the refined sensibilities of others, while consideration is practiced to avoid intruding on the rights and privileges of others.

In my view, respecting the rights of others is of paramount importance, both for our society at large and for individuals. In this section, I will focus briefly on the positive effect that considerate behavior can have on our own lives.

First, considerate behavior is infectious. By being concerned for the rights of others, we increase the likelihood that others will respect our rights as well. Secondly, being considerate of others can give us a sense of self-respect and self-esteem. I will give five examples of ways in which we can be considerate of others. In some of these examples, your only immediate reward for behaving in this way will be your own good feelings about yourself. However, in some of the examples, I will illustrate how this behavior can pay immediate dividends in terms of happiness, good will, convenience, or safety.

1. Let them in !

Have you ever been in your car, trying to pull out of a parking lot or side street and into a lane of heavy traffic? Have you ever been frustrated and angry because no one slowed down to let you in? The next time you are one of the cars in the lane of traffic and you see another driver trying to get into the lane, slow down and motion them in. In return, you may get a smile and a wave of thanks. Seemingly an insignificant event, this small act of good will and the acknowledgement of it may surprise you in terms of the good feeling it can provide!

2 - Show them you are aware of their presence, too!

Have you ever been in your car, waiting for pedestrians to cross a street before you could continue on your way? Have the pedestrians ever walked very slowly - so slowly that you actually felt they were being deliberately defiant? Did that make you feel angry or intruded upon? The next time you are crossing a street and a car is waiting, quicken your pace a little. I am not suggesting that you give away your right to walk at a comfortable pace. You do not have to run. Just give the impression that you are aware of someone waiting and that you are not trying to delay them.

3 - Pitch in and do a little more than your share!

Have you ever noticed how people sometimes fail to pick up after themselves - even though it inconveniences others? There are many examples of this, some of which are crude. I will use one that is not so crude. If you work out in a gymnasium or health club, it is a sure bet that you have noticed that people often use weights and leave them around without bothering to put them back where the next person can find them. In a way, this is ironic. If someone is trying to build up or maintain their muscles, and is capable of lifting a weight eight or ten times, you would think they could lift it **one more time** and put it back in its place!

First, if you work out, replace your own weights. Secondly, before you leave, find two or three weights that you did not use, and return them to their proper place. It will serve as a good example to others. And, it should not be a major inconvenience to you. After all, lifting heavy things is what you went there for in the first place.

4 - Give the appearance of extra caution and safety

Have you ever noticed how people often drive their cars too fast in residential neighborhoods and apartment complex parking lots? It is really a pretty silly thing to do. When you are off the main road and almost home, there is nothing you can do to get home significantly faster.

The suggestion I am going to give has to do with situations when parents and their little children are near the side of the road. Parents typically become very nervous when cars whiz by at 30 or 35 miles per hour. And, as I have already said, driving 30 or 35 instead of 20 will not make any significant difference. So, when you are driving near children, relax, be patient, and meander along at 20 miles per hour, or even less. People nearby will feel more comfortable and appreciate your extra concern for their safety, and you will feel good about your own ability to be relaxed, patient, and cautious as well.

5 - Show them that fairness is more important than opportunism!

There are many times when we find ourselves standing in line - at the supermarket, bank, post office, airport, motor vehicle registry, et cetera. And, oftentimes people will be overly opportunistic and aggressive about getting their errands done first. That type of behavior does not foster good will among people.

Some banks, post offices and airports use an architectural device to ensure fairness. They have a roped-off waiting line set up in such a way that when an agent or teller is ready, they call for the next customer, and everyone is thus served in the order in which they arrived. It works well to ensure fairness, but in a way, it is sad that people need to have fairness imposed on them.

The next time you are in a situation in which there are separate lines, and your line moves faster than that of a person who was waiting before you, when your turn comes ask the person who had been waiting before you to go ahead of you, since they had been there first. It will surprise that person, and probably please them that you are willing to place fairness ahead of opportunism. You will hardly be inconvenienced for any significant amount of time, you will feel good about yourself, and you will have contributed toward good will.

These examples are but five from the myriad ways in which we can make a statement in favor of consideration. As I stated at the beginning, considerate behavior is infectious, and you may be making a significant contribution toward good will in your community. You will almost surely be contributing to your own self-esteem.

Assertive Communication Really Helps

Assertiveness is a popular word. Many of us want to learn to be more assertive, to stand up for our rights, and not to have others take advantage of us. Unfortunately, assertiveness has often been misunderstood. People have confused it with a "looking out for number one" attitude. Assertiveness does **not** mean always looking out for number one. It does **not** mean insisting on winning arguments. It does **not** mean being unwilling to compromise or negotiate.

What does it mean to assert yourself? To be assertive means to be aware of what is important to us, and to behave toward others in a way that is consistent with who we are, what we value, and what we want. To be assertive is to be honest and to be self-affirming. Assertive behavior is respectful behavior. It is respectful both of ourselves and of others, and is the type of behavior that gives us the best chance to achieve our goals and to maintain our self-esteem.

Some people are afraid of the idea of being assertive. They see it as unrefined or aggressive. I hope to explode that negative view of assertiveness and to replace it with a positive one.

First, let us dismiss the idea of refinement, because refinement is not truly the issue here. The most manipulative and aggressive acts may be performed in a socially refined manner. The most kind and appropriately assertive acts may be performed in a coarse or unrefined way. In conducting assertiveness training, I do not in any way encourage lack of refinement. If assertive behavior can be achieved in a refined way, that is great! But the goal is to be honest, direct, and self-affirming.

My remarks may cause you to recall some personal experiences. Perhaps you have witnessed someone hiding dishonest or unethical behavior behind a mask of social grace. If so, I will bet you found it to be doubly frustrating. You may have felt that their social grace made it difficult for you to be heard, or to demand fair treatment. If you have such a memory, then you will probably be receptive to the idea that honesty is even more important than refinement. To adopt an assertive philosophy is to regard honesty and integrity as the most important social graces.

People often confuse **aggressiveness** with **assertiveness**. I am often asked whether people can be **so assertive** that they become aggressive. I will make some distinctions among **unassertive**,

assertive, and **aggressive** behavior that will help you see that aggression is **not** "over-assertion." Aggression is a different type of behavior altogether.

For one thing, assertive behavior means we make choices for ourselves. To be unassertive is to let others choose for us, and to be aggressive is to impose choices on others.

To be assertive means to give our wants, needs, and goals a high priority, while still respecting other people's rights. Assertive communication includes honest expression of our emotions. To be unassertive is to fail to promote our own goals, and to be emotionally dishonest. To be aggressive is to promote our own goals at the expense of other people.

I am going to give an example of a typical life conflict, and I will illustrate assertive behavior and its likely consequences. The dilemma I will use as an example is **not** a heavy, serious one. Just as a picture is said to be worth a thousand words, an example helps bring ideas to life.

Let us say that your neighbor Betty is not very good at taking care of material possessions. She comes over and says, "I'm having a party Saturday night. May I borrow some of your CDs? You know I have so few good ones."

First, let us look at unassertive behavior. You may not want Betty to take the records, and you say, "Gee, Betty, I'm really concerned about keeping them in good condition." Betty replies: "Oh, I promise to look after them." Although you know that Betty is not intentionally lying to you, you also know the following: A) Betty is **not** as responsible as she thinks she is. B) Many guests at the party will probably end up handling the CDs. And, C) Betty will be occupied by so many things that she cannot be expected to really look after the CDs. However, you are being unassertive, and despite your misgivings you say "Okay."

Several days later you get your CDs back, some scratched, and some with missing covers. You feel betrayed, angry, and used, but you keep those feelings to yourself. You give Betty "the cold shoulder" for a month. She does not know why you are treating her that way, and she feels rejected and hurt. Your lack of assertiveness has made no one happy.

Now let us look at aggressive behavior. When Betty asks to borrow the CDs, you say, "Are you kidding? . . . the way you take care of things?" Although hurt, Betty persists, and says: "But I'll take care of them." You say "Sure" with heavy sarcasm. Betty goes away and feels like a victim. Your CDs are safe, but you are left with the knowledge that you have victimized Betty. No one ends up happy as a result of aggressive behavior, either.

Now let us look at an assertive response. First, you have to decide what your goals are in the situation. Let us assume that you have the dual goal of protecting your CDs and your friendship with Betty. You say, "Betty, I wish I could help you, but CDs are so vulnerable at parties, and I really want to keep mine in good condition." Betty persists, and says, "I'll look after them. Really I will." You reply, "I know you mean that sincerely, Betty. But with all that goes on at a party, I really believe that there will be damage to my CDs despite your best efforts." Betty still persists: "I'll put up a sign over the stereo telling people to be careful." You say, "I value our friendship too much to risk the resentment I would feel if the CDs came back damaged. I'd like to help, but I'm going to say 'no'." Betty goes away feeling temporarily disappointed, but she knows you did not lie to her or make any ridiculous excuses.

Although she feels disappointed, she still feels respected, because you were honest. And, in a way she may even feel that you have affirmed your friendship by telling her you did not want to risk it due to resentment. As for you, you feel somewhat awkward at first. But, you respect yourself for not allowing yourself to be imposed on. (And your CDs are safe).

I hope that my illustration of the three styles - nonassertive, aggressive, and assertive - shows the emotionally destructive consequences of nonassertive and aggressive behavior. That is really the point. Unassertive and aggressive behaviors are emotionally damaging while assertive responses are likely to bring dignity and self-respect to all concerned.

In addition, assertiveness does not always mean getting something for ourselves or defending our life space from encroachment by others. Assertive behavior includes bringing important people closer to us. For instance, telling friends how much we appreciate them is an assertive act.

I hope that I have given you a positive and balanced view of assertiveness. The more people practice assertive communication and behavior, the fewer misunderstandings there will be. Honest, self-affirming communication can be a powerful force in your life.

Relating to Others when Time and Productivity are at Stake

With regard to both short-term tasks and long-range plans, it is helpful for us to be aware of how others affect our efforts, and to react accordingly.

1. Avoiding feelings of intrusion
on our time and space

Sometimes other people take up time that we truly feel we need for ourselves. It is crucial to assume full responsibility for yourself if you want to prevent someone from intruding on your time. If you want time to yourself to complete a project, and someone is making an implicit demand on you, you may avoid feelings of intrusion in any of the following ways:

> a. <u>Manipulation, or unclear message-giving</u>. You may look at your watch, shuffle papers on your desk, and hope that the person says, "Well, I'll let you get back to your work," and leave.
> b. <u>Assertion, or clear message-giving</u>. You may say, "I'm having difficulty paying full attention to you. I'm thinking of a project I'd like to complete, and I'd rather talk with you another time."
> c. <u>Changing our internal sentences</u>. You may decide that you would rather be with the person than work on the project, and be content with that decision. (Not to be content with that decision would lead you to feelings of intrusion.)

One concept helpful here is that of "risk versus reward." If you are considering dealing with another person in a way that might jeopardize the relationship in order to move a project forward, you may wish to assess the importance of the project (reward) versus the potential risk to the relationship.

2. <u>Enlisting the collaboration or cooperation of others</u>

Depending on our work style, cooperative efforts can have distinct advantages over individual work. A few are as follows:

<u>a. Added creativity</u>. Some projects that call for creativity or innovation can be handled better cooperatively. When you feel stuck, your work partner may help get things moving, and vice versa.

b. <u>Relief from temporary isolation</u>. Sometimes we can work alone to the point that we suffer from a loss of social contact. A compatible work partner can reintroduce companionship and humor into a work situation that may otherwise lack them.

c. <u>Relief from long-standing isolation</u>. Social isolation may be a more enduring theme in the lives of some people. Collaboration in work efforts can in some instances lead to long term friendships, which prevent feelings of social isolation in a more permanent way.

If you do want to involve another person as a collaborator on a project, you will need to assess your compatibility. It may not be possible to do so in advance of actually working together, so it may be sensible to avoid major projects for your first collaborative effort.

Section V

Materials and the Physical Environment

CHAPTER 18

ORGANIZING SPACE

Making Our Work Space Suit Us

Attention to physical appearance may be important for some of us. If a workspace is bleak or barren, and we find ourselves wandering out of it to gain a feeling of refreshment, our efficiency will be impaired. Adequate lighting will help us to work to our potential, as will proper temperature and ventilation. We probably work best when we are physically comfortable sitting (or standing) in our work place, and have all of our tools, files, papers, and paraphernalia within easy reach. We do much better when we enjoy being in our work place and feel as though we belong there.

Contending with Paper

We can use drawers, files, and supplies most effectively if they are divided and available according to priority. Here are a few of the ideas you may wish to consider relative to files, drawers, and supplies.

First, files are not just for offices anymore. Even in your home, you have the need to keep a variety of papers, including but not limited to utility bill statements, insurance documents, tax records, warranty cards, children's school records, voter registration cards, and credit card statements. Electronic records are not a good substitute for all other forms of record keeping. A file system may be simple or elaborate. It does not necessarily require you to purchase a piece of furniture. For many years I got by with a few cardboard boxes - the type sold by stationery stores for the purpose of file moving and storage. They may not be very attractive, but they are the perfect size and are useful. Even if you do want to purchase a file cabinet, as I eventually did, serviceable but inexpensive models are available. Regardless of how you do it, do set up a file and place it in a convenient location for your frequent use.

Establish a file folder for all papers you keep. Labeling all file folders will save waste of time thumbing through a bunch of them. Do not worry. If you discontinue that specific use of the folder, you can easily stick a blank label on it and re-use it.

Put a date on every piece of paper containing information. Preferably, put the source of the data also. In the future, you will be glad to know where and when you received the information. As an example, suppose that you are calling the phone company to set up or change your service. As you call, have a pad and pencil with you. When the service representative states his or her name, write it down at the top, along with the date and the name of the company. If you do not hear the name, ask for it. Then jot down the information you receive. After your call, place the sheet of paper with your notes into the appropriately labeled folder, and file it. If there is any future mix-up, you can not only state the information you received, but also the date and the source. This will be a helpful aid for you in unraveling the various snags that can occur in consumer and business situations.

If you need to stop midway through a project for any reason, such as a lack of resources, put this work in a file folder or tray marked "pending" and re-check these projects periodically. A small "stand up file" is a good way to keep folders currently in use. A good rule of thumb: store all papers vertically. Once papers, folders, et cetera, become buried in a horizontal pile, you may have difficulty retrieving them.

Try to work in such a way as to handle each piece of paper as few times as you can, once if possible. What this really implies is that it is to your advantage to make decisions about documents, rather than to repeatedly put a paper down on your desk and pick it up again.

Developing a good set of habits for handling the paperwork aspects of your life will save you a great deal of inconvenience, and even anguish. If you have ever said or thought the words "I am just not an organized person," be sure to add the words "so far." Being organized is not a trait with which we are born. It is a learnable set of skills. Moreover, it can help you to replace occasional or frequent feelings of being frustrated with feelings of competence and mastery.

CHAPTER 19

MAKING HOUSEHOLD TASKS EASY

The first task for the reader at this point is to decide whether you are satisfied with the degree to which you keep any of your various living spaces and work spaces organized. Many persons will admit to being dissatisfied with their housekeeping performance. However, many other persons will express antipathy toward housekeeping tasks, and in fact may consider good housekeepers to possess certain negative traits that may be described as "compulsive" or "persnickety." They may refer to good housekeepers by words such as "neat-nik", which are not entirely complimentary. It is clear that many persons regard organizational traits as a double-edged sword. The purpose of this section of the book is to help readers to regard organizational, housekeeping tasks as an activity that may be approached with moderation, and not on an all-or-none basis. Another purpose of this section is to advance certain useful suggestions for keeping our life spaces and workspaces better organized. The following are a few suggestions the readers may wish to consider:

"Do Ten Things"

This is a technique designed to combat the all-or-none behavior that may be characteristic of many people when it comes to housekeeping habits. Instead of assuming that any attempt to clean up or organize your space must be a thorough job (an assumption that very often leads to total neglect), I suggest that we may look at an office, apartment, or workshop and say "I will just do ten things before I go out, go to bed, leave for work, et cetera." We can put an old newspaper in the recycle bin and say "one"; we may bring a couple of used coffee mugs to the kitchen sink and say "two"; we may hang a coat in the closet and say "three"; we may put some throw cushions back on a sofa and say "four" - and so on until we have reached "ten." At ten, we stop. Yes, we do. We stop. It is possible that we may wish to continue once we have a good start, *BUT IT IS VERY IMPORTANT THAT WE GIVE OURSELVES PERMISSION TO STOP AT TEN.*

If we try to use the "do ten things" method to cajole ourselves into doing the entire job, we will avoid doing ten things just as we avoid tackling what seems to be a massive task. Occasional use of the "Do ten things" method may help us to keep our environment in reasonably good order without making it a major project.

"Clutter Zones" are Okay

If you believe that you can keep your entire living and working spaces completely neat and clutter-free, you are probably mistaken. Even the best organized of us cannot manage to keep after every credit card slip, business card, electric bill, store receipt, scarf, glove, product warranty card, screw driver, roll of electrical tape, tape measure, voter registration card, and letter from Mom. The idea of the "clutter zones" method is **not** to **avoid** the clutter, but to **limit** and **manage** the clutter. A nice little wicker basket on top of a bookcase in the living room will do nicely for the product warranty cards, letters from Mom, store receipts, et cetera. A cardboard carton in or near a closet will be fine for the pliers, rolls of electrical and duct tape, screwdriver, and flashlight batteries. A cardboard carton in the trunk of your car will handle the flashlight, road map, spare change, and a half-roll of toilet paper.

Moderation is the key. If you have too many planned clutter zones, you have accomplished nothing. If your clutter containers are too large, you have accomplished nothing. When the clutter zones become full, or full enough that items can be lost in them, it is time to spend a few minutes purging them with a round of "Do ten things." Skillful use of clutter zones can help you stay reasonably neat and reasonably organized with moderate effort.

The "Nutcracker Suite"

You can do your everyday strategic life maintenance tasks with a sense of hurry, frenzy, and distaste, or you can accomplish them with some relaxation, grace, and style. It is up to you and your imagination. You can attack your housekeeping tasks the way a baseball player tries to steal a base, or you can address the tasks the way a dancer performs in the Nutcracker Suite. If you believe that it is *impossible* for you to imagine that your house-keeping tasks are part of an elegant, graceful dance - *impossible* that they can be accomplished with pleasure and grace instead of frenzy and displeasure, then you are the victim of the critical capacity of your conscious mind. If you decide to suspend the critical capacity of your conscious mind for the establishment of creative thinking, then perhaps you *can* address those tasks in a completely different frame of mind. When you stop to think of the percentage of time during the remainder of your life in which you will - like it or not - be involved in what I usually call "practical, strategic life maintenance tasks," you will perceive that it may be in your best interest to try this method.

Here is my favorite way to teach someone to play "Nutcracker Suite." Decide on three tasks to perform. These are to be routine tasks that you can do in less than five minutes, and during which you typically feel rushed, uncomfortable, or "scattered."

Take an insulated, narrow neck bottle, such as a thermos bottle. It must be a bottle that has a distinctly changing sound as it is filled with water from a faucet. Stand in front of the kitchen sink with the thermos in one hand and your other hand on the tap. Take four to six slow, deep breaths. Close your eyes. Open the tap and listen carefully to the tone slowly whooshing up the scale as the thermos fills. In one smooth motion, close the tap so that you have turned off the water at the moment the thermos is full. Practice this procedure a few times, until you have achieved a smooth, pleasurable sense of coordination of the sound of the bottle filling and the feeling of turning off the tap. I will repeat that last instruction. *Practice this procedure a few times, until you have achieved a smooth, pleasurable sense of coordination of the sound of the bottle filling and the feeling of turning off the tap.* Take four to six additional slow, deep breaths. Do your three tasks. Do not ask "why?" Just enjoy a novel set of feelings as you perform your three tasks.

Section VI
Personal Finance

CHAPTER 20

CAN MONEY BUY HAPPINESS?

Is money important?

It would be pretty difficult to argue convincingly that money is not important. Almost everything we live in, transport ourselves with, eat, drink, and entertain ourselves with is available only through the accepted medium of exchange - money. To argue that money is not an important factor in life would be ignoring the facts.

Is money the crucial factor in happiness?

The former radio and television personality Edward R. Morrow once did a study of happy Americans. This information is anecdotal. I have not seen or read any official report describing his study, so I cannot determine whether it was a valid study in the way in which we psychology types like to see validity. But I found his results to be intriguing, and I believe he was onto something. He discovered that the happiest Americans are people who live within sight of a mountain or a body of water. Money, physical beauty, material possessions, athletic ability, political power ... none of those factors were mentioned.

Are the best things in life really free ?

So the saying goes, and I believe it. However, I also believe the following:

If we do not have the needed leisure time and freedom from worry, then we may not be in a frame of mind to enjoy the best things in life.

Thus, although the best things in life themselves are free, we need at least a certain amount of money to enjoy them. What are the "best things in life"? Here are five of my personal choices:

1. Friendship is a deep joy when it has developed to the point that:
    a) You can express yourself without fear of rejection;
    b) You can count on your friend to help you when you are in need;
    c) You are willing, with no sense of inconvenience, to help your friend when s/he is in need; and
    d) Distance does not seriously compromise the relationship.

2. Laughter is one of the best things in life. I am happy that stand-up comedy has made such a strong comeback. Granted, not all humor is kind, gentle, and respectful. Still, there is nothing like a good laugh for pure pleasure. Humor can help us to put things into perspective and see the lighter side of troublesome issues. There are even those who contend, apparently with some justification, that laughter increases the effectiveness of the human immune system.

3. The beauty of nature is one of the best things in life. The aforementioned study by Edward R. Morrow emphasizes this idea. Sunsets and sunrises are among my favorites, and there are numerous beautiful views in nature, such as starlit skies, mountains, bodies of water, big spreading trees, and little gurgling brooks.

4. Love and romance are among the best things in life. Most individuals hope for a relationship in which all or most of the following are present:

    a) Companionship, and mutual enjoyment of pastimes;

    b) Mutual respect for one another's abilities and resourcefulness;

    c) Mutual physical attraction and pleasure;

    d) Shared values, and a similar way of understanding the world;

    e) Good will, characterized by a genuine desire to enhance one another's self-esteem;

    f) Similar practical goals; and

    g) Compatibility of emotional needs.

If we are fortunate enough to enjoy such a romance, we undoubtedly place it among the best things in life.

5. Music, combined with the relaxation to really experience and enjoy it, is one of the best things in life. Many readers probably remember the musical piece "Night on Bald Mountain" by Mussorgsky. (It is the piece illustrated with the Halloween scene in Walt Disney's *Fantasia*). After the piece has reached its climax, there is a hauntingly beautiful sequence, featuring a flute. It is only one of a number of examples I could give of musical sequences that are so beautiful, or so spirited and lively, as to be among the best things in life.

However, have you ever had the experience of listening to music, and suddenly realizing that the music is over and that you had not really heard it because you were worried about something? Of course you have. And worry, sometimes over a practical matter that could be helped with money, can also take away or limit your enjoyment of romance, the beauty of nature, laughter and even friendship.

I know there are people who will argue that a joy such as listening to recorded music can only be appreciated if it is heard on an exquisite, expensive stereo. In the final analysis there is a difficulty evaluating other people's experiences. However, I have personally experienced a state of joy while listening to music played on an inexpensive stereo, and I have seen people with $10,000 stereos who were so busy making adjustments and acting in a generally restless fashion that it was hard to infer any pleasure or joy in their experience.

So are the best things in life free? I definitely believe they are. However, we probably need a relaxed, comfortable emotional frame of mind to enjoy the best things in life. Moreover, freedom from worry over finances, plus leisure time to enjoy those "best things in life," does require some mastery over money matters. At some point in our lives, freedom from work gained through our savings and investments may be a necessary ingredient for us to truly enjoy some of the best things in life.

CHAPTER 21

WHO IS IN CONTROL? ARE YOU?

There are many ways in which people lose control of their own fate and instead become caught up and controlled by forces outside their control. Money and materialism are in the forefront of those forces. Consider the plight of one of countless young individuals caught in a web of their own device.

Glenn graduated from college and began a career as a teacher. He identified two main goals for himself: making a direct contribution to the lives of others and living a comfortable, reasonably stress-free lifestyle. "Money and material possessions are secondary," he asserted. Soon he was ensconced in a comfortable teaching job and earning a decent salary. He got along well with the school administration, enjoyed his community, and felt that life was good. He enjoyed simple, relatively inexpensive activities such as hiking and jogging, and was content to live in a modest apartment and drive a used car.

Gradually and without a conscious decision to do so, Glenn changed certain financial and material aspects of his lifestyle. Having had to repair his car a few times during a severe winter, he decided that he did not want the risk of missing work, so he purchased a new car. He bought a $28,000 car instead of an $18,000 car, having been influenced by the salesperson's pitch. Glenn then received an offer of an administrative position in the school department. Although this would conflict with his stated goal of providing direct service, the added money and challenge drew him into accepting. He also bought a home. As so many people do, he listened to the sales person's encouragement to buy as expensive a home as he could qualify for, and ended up purchasing a more elaborate home than he had intended. Although he had never really coveted the features that made his new home more expensive, he was somehow talked into the purchase.

Glenn's life continued to change. After evening administrative meetings he often found himself in restaurants that he had previously thought of as extravagant and unnecessary, and his credit card balance grew surprisingly large. Eventually, in a gradual process that gained momentum as it went along, Glenn took on a large set of fixed expenses.

Then the character of his job changed. An era of fiscal difficulties caused extreme friction between the school administration and teachers. Glenn found himself having teachers, who he felt were his natural colleagues, as adversaries, with resulting loss of friendships, and tension in the friendships that survived. Sunday nights found him nervous and full of dread about the workweek ahead. He fervently wished that he could resign his administrative job and go back to teaching and a simpler lifestyle, but he felt tied into his administrative job because of his overgrown fixed expenses. He thought back about the feelings he had had when he began his career, and he wondered how he could have let himself fall into this trap.

This scenario is not a fiction. And it is but one of countless stories of persons whose material lifestyles gradually grow out of proportion to their original intentions, leaving them feeling trapped and unable to reassert control of their own destinies.

The changes in Glenn's life were so gradual and so natural! And, the allure of more expensive housing, transportation and entertainment is reinforced by so many other people and by so many cultural norms! Is it reasonable to expect anyone to resist those forces and to maintain a less expensive lifestyle - one that would allow a return to lower paying employment in order to escape stress and to reassert lifestyle preferences?

The important question is not whether it is "reasonable," according to some hypothetical standard. The question is whether *you* want to run the risk of encountering the consequences that Glenn faced due to making choices similar to his. There is a movement, or a school of thought, developing at this time. It is known as "voluntary simplicity," and its ideas are very similar to those I am advocating in this book. Cutting back on some materialistic expenses - particularly those that are lower in your personal or your family's value system - can pay a bonus in terms of freedom.

Life is a game of "choices and consequences." Each of us plays the game and, in the final analysis, it is a solitary game. We alone are responsible for the choices, and we alone must live with the consequences. However, with a modicum of forethought, some examination of your personal values, and application of the ideas found in this book, you can achieve a great deal for yourself. You can use money to your advantage, put materialism in its proper perspective for your value system, and achieve a sense of personal mastery over your life.

CHAPTER 22

WHY INVEST FOR THE FUTURE ?

Live for today! (Right?)

I am sure most readers will recall the fable about the ant and the grasshopper. It was summer time and the grasshopper was lounging around, playing the fiddle, and enjoying life during the good weather. The ant was toiling away, building an underground home for the winter and storing food. The grasshopper said to the ant, "Why don't you rest for a while, and enjoy Nature's bounty?" The ant replied, "I would rather work now and be safe, warm, and well fed when winter comes."

When winter did come, the ant was as safe, warm, and well fed as he had planned to be. The grasshopper, almost dead from starvation and cold, came to the ant's door and asked to be let in. The dutiful ant did indeed allow the grasshopper to enter. The grasshopper was saved from destruction by the ant's work and planning.

You may think that this is merely a fable, but there are many grasshoppers among us. Many persons do indeed have a "live for today" philosophy of life. I am sure they believe in their philosophy of life as fervently as did the grasshopper in the fable. Below

I will repeat a statement that I have heard from persons who did not want to focus on investing for the future. I will follow their statement with my perspective on why their reasoning is flawed.

> If I have money today, I want to use it today. Life is too uncertain. If I save my money, who knows if I will even be alive to enjoy it in the future? And if I am alive in the future, I'll have no regrets because I'll have lived life fully.

Yes, it is true that life does have its uncertainties, including the uncertainty of how long we will even be alive to benefit from saving and investing a portion of our money. However, the future that a person is referring to when they make the above statement is the *imagined future*. However, what if we do in fact go on living? Then, *that imagined future becomes the living present*, and all the *previous indulgence becomes the dead past*. I have never met or heard of any person ever feeling okay about an impoverished living present just because they indulged themselves in the dead past. No, our living present is too important. *And if you go on living, then today's imagined future will have become your living present.* You had better prepare for it financially.

Retirement will not be easy !

Recent economic analysis has revealed some startling news about prospects for today's workers. One depiction of this analysis was described two decades ago in an article by Clint Willis in the June, 1991 issue of *Money* magazine. Willis quotes economist Richard Michel of the Urban Institute:

> *Today's retirees were a lucky exception to history. Your parent's generation was all but guaranteed a comfortable retirement by a succession of breaks during their working years.*

Michel's analysis revealed that in the 1950's and 1960's, when to-day's retirees were buying their first homes and starting their families, family income after inflation rose rapidly, housing prices as a percentage of family income were low, and social security benefits increased at a rate considerably higher than inflation. Then in the 1970's and 1980's, when that generation was investing for retirement, stock and bond yields were high by historical standards. This happy confluence of events has given many people financial stability in retirement.

However, the next generation will *not* be the beneficiaries of such good luck. Housing prices as a percentage of family income are much higher. It is unlikely that social security retirement benefits will rise faster than inflation, and the buying power of family income is actually decreasing for the overwhelming percentage of American families. Savings rates are low and family purchasing power is slipping. The frightening conclusion of Deborah Chollet, Associate Director of the Center for Insurance Research at Georgia State University, is:

**Some workers who have never been poor
will be poor in retirement.**

From an individual point of view, the answer to this developing dilemma is not despair, but rather an informed and systematic approach to personal budgeting and to investment for your future. Analysts estimate that you will need at least 80% of your pre-retirement income in order to be comfortable during retirement. If you have extensive travel or recreational plans, you may need 100% of your pre-retirement income, or even more. Social security cannot be counted upon to replace more than about 30% of pre-retirement income for most of today's workers. It is in your best interest to plan for your future. If you are over 30 years of age and not yet setting aside at least 20% of your income for retirement, you may be in danger. You may wish to seek advice from a financial service professional to assess the adequacy of your current plan. Current estimates are that eighty percent of today's workers will have less than fifty percent of the income they will need for a comfortable retirement.

Another sobering fact is that American households have less disposable income and more debt than ever before. In the April 1996 issue of Money magazine it was reported that in the previous two years, installment debt increased by one-third and total household debt skyrocketed from 80 to 93 percent of annual disposable income. These numbers were alarming, and should have served as a wake-up call to those who understood their implication. More recent events led to a tremendous real estate bubble in the 2005-2008 era, with well-documented and tragic consequences.

Individuals, couples and families are going to need to come to terms with their day-to-day cash flow. They will have to learn to budget their money more effectively, spending for those items that, according to their values and priorities, enrich their lives, and strictly limiting their spending on items that do not enhance their lives but that do waste potential investment dollars. They will then have to utilize the cash flow that they have freed up to invest in financial products to secure their futures. The BUDGET ACCOUNT SYSTEM briefly described in chapter 24 will enable you to achieve mastery over your cash flow in a way that will feel easy and natural, not tedious, painstaking and boring.

A TALE OF TWO COUPLES

Author's note: For the sake of clarity and simplicity, in describing the financial lives of the two couples I will ignore inflation and will discuss their finances as though a dollar twenty-five years ago and a dollar today are the same dollar. This is, of course, not true due to inflation, but this just an illustration, and describing it in terms of constant dollars will make it easier.

The Setting

Al and Kim are best friends with Bill and Sue. All four of these individuals are fifty-five years old, and they have been friends for more than twenty-five years. Kim and Sue went to school together and both received their teaching certificates at the age of thirty. They were both hired by Sleepy Valley High School, and have worked there and have been friends ever since. Al and Bill met when they were in orientation training together at Ace Tool and Die, where they work in technical sales. They have also been friends since then. Al and Kim were married just a few weeks after Bill and Sue's wedding, and the two couples' lives have paralleled one another's in almost every respect ever since then.

Both couples bought similar homes after one year of marriage, had two children at the same times, enjoyed the same recreational pursuits, and went on similar summer vacations. The money management habits of the two couples were almost identical as well.

The Finances

There were only three differences in the spending patterns of these two couples:

1) Both couples are two car families, and both take loans to buy new cars, and trade them every five years. However, Al and Kim have always bought the least expensive of the reliable cars, cars that as of this writing would sell for approximately sixteen to eighteen thousand dollars. Bill and Sue, on the other hand have always preferred cars closer to the higher end of the expense spectrum, cars that as of this writing would cost about twenty-six to twenty-eight thousand dollars. Not only are the monthly payments on Bill and Sue's cars higher than Al and Kim's, but their comprehensive automobile insurance premiums are higher, as are their local property taxes. I will leave out the calculations in the service of brevity, but let us estimate that between the purchase price, financing costs, insurance premiums and property taxes, Bill and Sue's monthly car expenses are $1154, compared with $700 for Al and Kim.

2) All four of these individuals really like to take a break in their workday by going out for lunch, or at least sending out for restaurant food. However, Al and Kim's concept is that if they bring their lunch from home twice a week, the three times they go out will be much more of a treat. Bill and Sue, on the other hand, reject the idea of ever making their lunches at home and bringing them to work. They prefer to eat restaurant

food for lunch every working day. Including tax and tip, the average lunch out for these individuals is ten dollars. Bringing lunch from home costs two dollars per lunch. Figuring an average of twenty working days per month, Bill and Sue spend $400 per month on lunches, compared to $272 for Al and Kim.

3) Both couples enjoy restaurant dining on Friday and Saturday nights. They have always believed that as hard working individuals they deserve to treat themselves to some luxuries. Bill and Sue like to order elaborate items on the menu, items that would as of this writing cost an average of $24.00 per person. Al and Kim, on the other hand, tend to "read the menu from right to left," and satisfy themselves with less elaborate entrees with an average cost of $12.00. Al and Kim are not cheap people. They tip as though they had ordered more expensive entrees, but between the entree price and tax, they save thirteen dollars per person per night out. Al and Kim spend an average of $36 per evening dining out; Bill and Sue spend an average of $62 per evening. Since they go out to dinner an average of eight times per month, Al and Kim experience a startling $208 per month saving compared to Bill and Sue's monthly dining out expenses.

To summarize, Al and Kim have all the same tastes, styles and expenses as Bill and Sue but for three exceptions: cars, lunches, and weekend dining out.

Let us look at some of the monthly expenses for Bill & Sue, and for Al & Kim, relative to automobiles, lunches and dining.

Expense	Bill & Sue	Al & Kim
Automobile	$1154	$ 700
lunches	$ 400	$ 272
dining	$ 496	$ 288
T O T A L	$2050	$1260

There is a $790 difference between these two couples in their total monthly outlays for the three expenses. In all other ways, their spending habits are identical. Moreover, what do Al and Kim do with their $790 per month savings? They send the entire $790 every month to a mutual fund family and have it allocated among stock mutual funds. For twenty-five years they have sent in their check regardless of whether the stock market has been rising or falling, using a strategy known as "dollar cost averaging." We will skip any detailed discussion of which funds Al and Kim have invested in, what the individual funds' performances were, and what the effect has been of their particular asset allocation strategy. We will just assume that their funds have performed in line with the indexes, and that even after deducting money from their funds each April to pay taxes on the dividends and capital gains distributions, they have averaged an eight-percent annual return. If you invest one dollar per year at eight percent for twenty-five years, you will end up with $78.95. You can look this up in any compound interest table. Thus, a $9,480 annual investment ($790 X 12 = $9,400) would grow to $748,446 - just under three-quarters of a million dollars.

As the years went by, Al, Kim, Bill and Sue spent a great deal of time together. They dined together at least once each weekend, vacationed together in the summers, and attended social and recreational events together. They shared with one another their feelings about work, child rearing and life in general. In almost all respects, they were photocopies of one another. The only discernible difference has been a desire on Al and Kim's part to save money on cars, lunches and dining out, and to invest the savings. Al and Kim have taken a great deal of gentle kidding from Bill and Sue over the years about these issues.

Over dinner in a restaurant, Bill would sometimes say "Al, tell me the truth. Wouldn't you rather be eating the surf and turf that I'm having instead just broiled fish? Come on! Life is short! Live a little!" And Al would reply "I am living a little, Bill. The atmosphere and service in this restaurant, plus your good company, make this evening very enjoyable. Having an entree that costs twelve dollars more would not make it any more fun. I would rather invest the twelve dollars, Bill. Maybe someday Kim and I will want to buy a vacation home, or a boat, or even retire early. I'd rather save for something like that than to spend more on dinner."

Sue would sometimes chime in "Retire early? You know you love your work. We all do. We all plan to be productive workers, out there joining in the pulse of life every day, as long as we can. So why not spend a little more to enjoy life now, knowing that will be working and earning 'til we're 65 or 70?" And Kim would answer "You may be right, Sue. Going to work and being a part of things every day feels good. I would never want to retire early under these circumstances. But there have been a few times when I dreaded going to work for a while. I can imagine things getting so tough that I would want out. I'd like to save and invest just in case."

The two couples never did see eye to eye on Al and Kim's insistence on limiting their outlays in these three areas in order to invest for the future. So, Al and Kim put up good naturedly with Bill and Sue's kidding about their less expensive cars, their inexpensive homemade lunches twice a week, and their habit of ordering more modest entrees in restaurants.

The Crisis

Finally, though, events put these habits into an entirely different light. The working conditions changed both for Al and Bill at Ace Tool and Die and for Kim and Sue at Sleepy Valley High School. Al and Bill were both passed over for promotion to the position of marketing director, a position for which they agreed they were both qualified. The company put a younger man in the position. Al and Bill agreed that the new man favored other younger sales personnel, and they had feelings of injustice and frustration. Furthermore, the company took away some of Al and Bill's more lucrative accounts and made them into house accounts, taking their commissions from them and making them work much harder to try to maintain their compensation level. And that was just the tip of the iceberg. In a number of ways, the familiar working environment that Al and Bill had found comfortable, and in which they had felt competent and valued, began to feel more like a battlefield. Both men began to feel a great deal of physical tension at work, and to experience physical manifestations of the tension such as headaches, heartburn and stiff necks. They had psychological effects as well, including irritability, loss of pleasure in pastimes that had always been enjoyable, and a pervasive feeling of anxiety.

Matters were no better for Kim and Sue at Sleepy Valley High. Kim and Sue had also been passed over for promotion for positions as curriculum director and principal. The new persons in those positions demanded much more paperwork for purposes of accountability, and both Kim and Sue felt oppressed by the new regime. After they voiced their concerns in a staff meeting, they were called in by the principal and informed that charges of insubordination awaited any teachers who refused to keep up with the school's new accountability standards. For years, Kim and Sue had agreed that the school felt like a second family to them. Now they looked back at those idyllic times from what seemed like a maze of paperwork, political infighting and paranoia.

All four friends were miserable, and their time together was dominated by their discussions of how their work environments had deteriorated so badly, and about how unappreciated and betrayed they felt there. Changing jobs seemed to be a near impossibility. Al and Bill, with all their experience in technical sales, were in a specific industry that had dwindled, partially due to the exporting of many manufacturing functions to foreign countries. Companies in other industries were not interested in Al and Bill when they could hire younger personnel (although they would never have admitted that age was a consideration). And Kim and Sue were already at such a high pay scale with their years of service that transfer to another school department was very unlikely. All four individuals felt trapped, hopeless and miserably unhappy.

Two Different Endings

The couples went to their respective financial advisors to explore their prospects for early retirement. Kim and Sue participated in the municipal teacher's retirement system, and their twenty-five years of service entitle them to a retirement income of 50% of their pre-retirement salaries. However, they are not eligible (unless disabled) to begin to collect until the age of 60. That is five years away. Al and Bill's company dismantled its fixed benefit retirement plan years earlier and replaced it with a 401K plan. Al and Bill have been contributing to the plan for the past five years, but their company does not provide matching funds, and they do not have a great deal invested. Furthermore, they are not eligible to withdraw any monies from the plan without penalty until they reach the age of 59 and 1/2.

For Bill and Sue, the situation is grim. The advisor told them that they would have to trim their expenses so that Bill can maximize his contributions to his 401K. Furthermore, they will have to continue to work, at least until the age of 60 when they can both access their retirement plans, and possibly a year or two longer if they are to have the financial means they want in retirement. Bill and Sue feel trapped and desperate.

Al and Kim came away from their meeting with their financial advisor with the weight of the world lifted from their shoulders. Their advisor looked at their $748,446 of mutual fund investments. He told them that if this were their only financial means, he would advise them not to withdraw more than 4% per year, or $29,940, in order to be confident that they would not deplete their capital. However, since Kim's municipal teachers retirement benefits will be due in five years, plus Al's somewhat limited 401K monies in four and one-half years, he felt they can afford to begin immediately to withdraw 7.5%, or $56,133 per year, and then reduce their withdrawals when the other funds become available. He thus advised them to request a monthly check for $4,700 from the mutual fund company. This is not as much money as Al and Kim are used to living on, but they are positive they can find ways to cut expenses.

So just when Al and Kim felt that they could not emotionally tolerate their work one month longer, they wrote letters of resignation, giving two weeks' notice, and they left. Bill and Sue felt just as emotionally beaten down by their work situations, but they were not in a financial position to do anything about it - all because they had insisted on the importance to them of more expensive cars, restaurant lunches every day, and fancier entrees at dinner than those with which their friends had satisfied themselves. By placing savings and investments among their financial life strategies, Al and Kim were able to attain freedom at a crucial point in their lives. Their friends Bill and Sue had not been as concerned about the future, and felt trapped and desperate at the same juncture. The "Al and Kim method" could very well end up playing a major part in *your future happiness* and convenience as well.

CHAPTER 24

EFFECTIVE CASH FLOW MANAGEMENT

Have you ever received an income tax refund or some other extra funds? Have you ever identified a good use for it, deposited the money into your regular checking account, and then found before long that the money has been "absorbed into your regular cash flow"? Have you ever gone into debt for a vacation, and then had your pleasure diminished by worry about the expenses? Have you ever felt anxious while having your car looked at by a mechanic because you wondered where the money for a repair was going to come from? Have you ever had an opportunity to buy something you have been wanting, but felt uneasy because of thoughts about what other payments or expenses might be coming up?

If you answered "no" to **all** the above questions, then you either:

A. have enough wealth not to worry about expenses;
B. already have a systematic approach to your finances;
C. have a relaxed, "devil-may-care" attitude about money; or
D. resist admitting to some of your money problems.

If you answered "yes" to one or more of the questions, then you can probably benefit from applying a good system for cash flow. And, you **do not** even have to organize **most** of your spending. You will be amazed at how simple and elegant a good cash flow system can be.

The Problem with Typical Budgeting

Articles and books about personal money management are easy to find. Most of those methods start by asking you to look back through your financial records of the past year -- check books, savings accounts, credit card receipts, et cetera -- and to write down every dollar you can account for. The idea is for you to discover where you have spent all your money for the past year. However, there is a risk to such a painstaking approach. It could make you so fatigued that you might give up the idea of budgeting altogether.

After suggesting the difficult process of analysis, the typical budgeting system suggests that you determine the monthly amount you can afford for each major category of expenditure. For instance, it may be suggested that you set a limit for how much money you spend each month on going out for lunch. Theoretically, that may be a good idea. *But, most of us don't want to keep track of exactly how much we have spent.* And, we don't want to feel limited. Even if we do realize that we must **be** limited; we just do not want to **feel** limited. Furthermore, we do not want to go through the detailed process of writing down the amount we spend on lunch every day. Face it: most of us just do not want to organize our lives and our finances in ways which feel too detailed, tedious, and constricting.

"Regular" and Intermittent Expenses

"Regular" expenses are those we have every month. Rent (or house payment) is a regular expense. Utility bills are regular expenses. Buying groceries is a regular expense, as are gasoline for the car, toiletries, and buying a newspaper.

If all our expenses were regularly-occurring such as these, we would probably develop a "feel" for our cash flow, and would plan accordingly.

Why are your attempts to manage your money "by feel" doomed to failure? The problem is **not** the regularly occurring expenses described above. The "monkey wrenches in the machinery" are the expenses that occur irregularly, occasionally, or "unpredictably." The reason I put the word "unpredictably" in quotes is that *they are not really unpredictable.* They just feel that way.

Which expenses am I talking about? I am talking about bills for automobile repair, automobile insurance, vacations, holiday gifts, life insurance premiums . . . . . that kind of thing. If these expenses were spread out evenly month-to-month, you would not experience the false build-ups and the quick drops in your checking account that make your finances confusing. You would be able to come to terms with them along with your regular expenses. However, they do not, and they throw your financial awareness and planning into confusion.

Think about the following scenario, and see if it helps get across the idea of how intermittent expenses confuse our thinking:

You are in a restaurant, sitting back with an after-dinner drink, having just savored shrimp cocktail, filet mignon, salad, and wine. And, best of all, you have not spent a dime

. . . . yet. However, before you leave, you are handed a check with some big numbers on it. Before paying the check in the restaurant, you would not kid yourself into thinking that you were eating for free, would you? And when the waiter hands you the check, you do not say *"Oh, no!! What a stroke of bad luck !! A check to pay !! "*

But you may have a very similar reaction in other situations. Let us consider the example of auto repair. Imagine you have driven your car for the last 3 months without a single repair expense. You are saving money, right? . . . . **WRONG !**

Almost all car repairs result from normal wear and tear, **not** bad luck. Since you have driven your car for three months, you are due for lubrication (oil, oil filter, and chassis). That is thirty dollars. And, while driving for three months you have also used up approximately:

> $28 worth of your car's tires
> $20 worth of your car's exhaust system
> $20 worth of your car's brakes
> $20 worth of your car's alternator and battery
> $25 worth of your car's air conditioning system
> $ 2 worth of your car's thermostat
> $20 worth of your car's radiator and water
>   pump
> $20 worth of your car's front end
> $15 worth of your car's clutch and/or
>   transmission, and
> $10 worth of your car's fuel injection system.

That is $180. Add in the $30 for lubrication and we are at $210 for three months, an average of $70 per month. That is probably a good approximation of what it costs you to maintain your car. Of course, you may have gone six months now with no repairs - just gasoline and lubrication. But eventually, just when you least expect it . . . . wham ! ! You are going to have auto repair expenses. It is inevitable. Moreover, six or seven hundred dollars of car repair expenses following six months of "good luck" would not be unusual.

For the six months that you enjoy trouble-free driving, you may approach the end of each month with $70 left over. As you approach the end of the month, you feel okay financially. You look in your checkbook, and the balance seems good for this time of month. With no expenses in sight, you indulge in a luxury (an extra dinner out, art print, exquisite brand of scotch, gift for a loved one, or tickets to a cultural or sporting event). After enjoying your extra $70 per month for six months, you have spent 6 X $70 = $420. When you are "hit with the unexpected car repair bill," you have to put it on a charge card. You are frustrated. You worry about paying it off. And, worst of all, you may feel incompetent!

I hope that this example conveys to you how intermittent expenses throw off our ability to manage cash flow by feel, and convinces you of the enormous savings in terms of emotional energy that we can experience by an effective cash flow system.

Picking out the Signal from the Noise

One of the key concepts here is that almost all of us go by feel when it comes to budgeting. I am not going to ask you to change that. I am convinced that with the addition of a simple system for handling intermittent expenses, you can handle your cash flow "by feel," and do it successfully.

The problem with budgeting by feel is that you do not have a clear signal - a clear indication of where you are financially. The concept of telling the signal from the noise was originally radio terminology, but has been borrowed in statistics and other fields. In personal finances, the "signal" refers to your true financial status relative to income, cash on hand, and obligations. "Noise" refers to the many intermittent expenses that cause your checkbook balance to fluctuate in such a way that your end-of-the-month cash on hand does not give you a true signal.

The Cookie Jar Approach

Think back to the problem we had with the $420 car repair. Imagine that we had a cookie jar in a cupboard, with a label that read "auto repair." Suppose that every month after receiving our paycheck we had put seventy dollars into the cookie jar, and had reserved the money for that purpose. As we approached the end of each month, we may not have felt as financially comfortable, and may *not* have felt good about making the extra luxury expenditures described previously. As the cash built up to four hundred twenty dollars during our six months of trouble-free driving, we may have rejected the conclusion that we were the beneficiaries of good luck. We may have resisted the temptation to spend our auto repair money on something else. When the repair bills materialized, we would have been ready. We would have felt competent, clever, and responsible, rather than anxious or put upon. This sense of mastery and of freedom from worry is worth a great deal. You can have it without using a tedious, detailed cash flow system.

So Much For Car Repair
Is There More?

Clearly, car repairs are not the only type of intermittent expense that can throw our "seat of the pants calculations" off. For instance, there are auto insurance, vacations, holiday gifts, life insurance, professional dues, home repair, and others. The illustration with the cookie jar is just an analogy. The concept is real, and you may use an equivalent procedure.

The important idea is for you to. 1. estimate most of your intermittent expenses, 2. calculate what the expense is on a monthly basis, and 3. set aside the appropriate amount of funds for each expense at the beginning of the month. That way, as you progress through the month, there will be no "false build-ups" and no "quick drops" due to intermittent expenses. When you get a feel for your financial position, your "feel" may be an accurate one. The signal comes through, undisturbed by the noise. The unpleasant surprises that might otherwise throw you into disarray will be taken care of.

This discussion has given you some of the basic concepts about how to avoid tedious, boring budget systems and to set up an easy, elegant cash flow system for yourself. For a detailed discussion, illustrated with fifteen true-to-life vignettes, you may want to read my book entitled: *Cure Your Money Ills: Improve Your Self Esteem through Personal Budgeting.*

Section VII

Exercise

CHAPTER 25

OVERCOMING AVOIDANCE OF EXERCISE

If President John F. Kennedy were alive today, he might be discouraged by some of the aspects of American culture that he would see. However, one thing he would be very proud of is the emphasis in American society, at least among a portion of the population, on physical fitness. Fitness has become a strong theme among many persons in our culture. Sometime in the 1980's, jogging suits and running shoes became proper attire for many public places other than athletic facilities. Women's athletics have taken their place along with men's athletics. (It is illegal in public education to ignore women's athletics in favor of men's in terms of spending of tax dollars). The ideal of female beauty, once a softer, less athletic one than that for men, has changed. In countless ways, we are showing that physical fitness is important to us.

Exercise has become accepted as a legitimate preventative measure for such conditions as hypertension and heart disease. Research in the field of immunology has shown that physical exercise can enhance the effectiveness of the human immune system. In addition, exercise is sometimes referred to as "America's best arthritis medicine."

There are many popular forms of exercise. In my view, there are FIVE major types of exercises:
- Strength training
- Cardiovascular exercise
- Balance training
- Flexibility training
- Mind/body integration.

I do not intend to help you choose an exercise program. Your own age, level of fitness, tastes, lifestyle, and physical limitations will guide you. There are a number of professionals in physical education, physical therapy, chiropractic, osteopathy, and orthopedics to turn to if you want help in planning a training regimen. **My intention is to help you carry out the program you choose.**

The best-designed workout in the world will not help you if you avoid it. This may appear to be a simple minded assertion, but years of experience working with people has impressed me with how often people miss their workouts. Moreover, most of the missed workouts are due not to illness, injury, or any unavoidable cause, but rather to emotional and behavioral causes. Kim's account may be a good illustration:

> I love to stay fit. And, I've always liked to push myself to higher levels of fitness. My main activities are running, weight lifting and softball. Softball is just for fun, but running and weight lifting are serious training for me. But, they are not quite as serious as they used to be, and because of that I am doing better at them than ever before.
>
> Before I learned to manage things better, I used to be very rigid about always making my workouts tougher and never backing off. For example, when

I started running for fitness at age 22, I used to jog a mile, and I did not time it. I began to wonder how long it took me, so I brought a watch along. In retrospect, that was a big mistake! I first timed myself at seven minutes and forty-five seconds for the mile. I kept bringing the watch to see how I would do as I continued to train. After a while, it became a challenge for me to do better than I had the day before. Within three months, I had my time for the mile down to 6:30, and I was sure I would be running the mile in under 6:00 very soon.

Then, one day I was not feeling very well. I was not actually sick, just a little tired. I thought about how much energy I had to expend to run the mile in six minutes, and I could not handle the idea, so I just skipped it altogether. That became the pattern. I was afraid to do my running on days when I did not feel my very best, because I was afraid of "running a bad time." And, even when I felt fine physically, I dreaded the run because of the pressure I was putting on myself.

Finally, it was explained to me what I was doing to myself. I was doing my running less often, and I was not enjoying it at all. I therefore just totally dropped the idea of timing. I have not brought a watch with me since then. If I am feeling particularly strong and enthusiastic, I run harder, but I do not concern myself about the actual time. If I am not feeling my best, I run more slowly. But, I do my running anyway, since there is no pressure to meet any standard. I am in better condition than ever, and I enjoy the activity again.

Kim's story illustrates a very important point for individuals who want to keep up an exercise program for fitness. You may want to measure your performance, and to improve in some way, but there are dangers involved. First, you may lose your intrinsic enjoyment of the activity due to the pressure to improve. Second, you could easily begin to dread your exercise routine, and to avoid it. You will be much more physically fit if you establish a moderate exercise routine and perform it regularly than if you establish a more demanding routine and avoid it frequently.

Phil has a story that will also be instructive:

> I love to work out to stay in shape. I do some bicycling and brisk walking, but my main activity is weight training. I belong to a fitness center, and I go there three times a week to work out. My workouts are enjoyable, but it was not always that way.

> I started with a workout that consisted of twenty sets of exercises and that took me approximately 45 minutes. I stayed with this basic workout for several months, the only change being that I increased the amount of weight I was lifting on a few exercises. Then I had a few days in which I felt particularly strong and energetic, and I doubled up on a few exercises, bringing my total workout to 26 sets and approximately an hour. Once I had done this a few times I decided I should stick with the expanded routine. I even added 2 sets of 2 new exercises, bringing my session to 30 sets and an hour and twenty minutes.

> I was really excited about the progress I was making, but it did not last. I had made my routine so difficult that on my less energetic days I would

dread going to the fitness center. I began to miss workouts every time I had an excuse to do so. I started to feel guilty about the whole affair. Then, someone explained to me a more useful way to approach my fitness sessions. First, I cut my routine back to my original 20 sets, which took me about 45 minutes. Second, I told myself that if I felt really energetic for a day, a week, or even several weeks, I would allow myself to expand my workout during that period of high energy. But I would revert to the 20-set workout the very first time I found myself dreading the workout, or finding it unpleasant and burdensome. Third, I decided that if I started my routine and it felt tiresome and unpleasant instead of fun and rewarding, I would give myself permission to cut the workout short, shower, and leave. After I had made these decisions, I continued with the 20-set workout for several weeks. Then I had one of those energetic periods. I expanded the workout to 24 sets for two weeks. During my first workout of the third week, it began to feel tiresome, and I cut the session to 20 sets that very day. I did not "find any excuses" to miss any sessions the way I had in the past whenever I had expanded my routine. As far as giving myself permission to cut the workout short and leave early, I have used that only once, but it makes a big difference. I never have to dread the workout because I know I can allow myself to cut it short if it feels burdensome. I feel more confident than ever before that I will continue with my fitness program, because I have learned how to be flexible. Being flexible has made the whole endeavor feel more enjoyable, and I hardly ever miss a session.

Phil's story illustrates the following points:

1. Expanding an exercise program entails the risk that the workout will seem so difficult that you may avoid it altogether.

2. You can still take advantage of periods of especially high energy and increase your routine. If you are willing to revert to the "basic routine" at the first sign of fatigue or resistance, you will not be endangering the consistency of your workouts.

3. You will carry out your exercise routines more consistently when they feel like self-enhancement and not self-oppression. It would be helpful for you to give yourself "standing permission" to end a workout early. You will probably use this permission very rarely, as you can usually "get into it" once you have started working out. However, that permission will lower your resistance to going to the gym on days when you do not initially feel energetic. Therefore, permission to end early will have the net result of fewer missed workouts.

Section VIII

Social Life

S ocial life is a very broad and complicated topic. The degree to which your social life is important to you is a matter of individual taste and lifestyle, and is to some degree rooted in personality factors that were being formed when you were very young. There is no space in a book such as this one to try to explain human social behavior in general, or even to attempt to create a multi-faceted model that would provide a separate set of suggestions for each of a number of personal/social styles.

Therefore, I will operate under the assumption that social life is important to you, and I will emphasize the following point:

The suggestions that follow in this chapter are **not** "the right and proper way to enhance a social life." They are merely suggestions that may prove helpful to many persons. However, your personal tastes and style must be the determining factor in your selection of ways to enhance your social life.

CHAPTER 26

LET THEM KNOW YOU THINK OF THEM!

Cards for All Occasions

Life today is more complicated than ever before. An increasing number of American families have two working adults, leaving fewer "person-hours" for various activities and social graces. Therefore, you may inadvertently neglect persons whom you may truly feel are important to you. Demands on our time may make it difficult to attend to the task of sending cards on birthdays, anniversaries, and other occasions -- unless we learn an efficient method to do so.

I will suggest a method for remembering people on special occasions, a method I have found to be fast, inexpensive and successful. The small investment in time and effort may pay big dividends in terms of helping you to feel connected to and appreciated by others.

First, you need to maintain two reference materials: 1) a list of dates and 2) a directory of names and addresses. The list can be handled on a single page (see Appendix B). Appendix B is simply a page divided into 12 boxes, each labeled with the name of a month of the year. When you learn the birthday or anniversary of someone you care enough about to send a card to, write the date and name in the appropriate box. Use a somewhat abbreviated style. For instance, if Laura Beckwith's birthday is November 17, write "11/17 - Laura B." *Keep this list in a file folder in an accessible place and refer to it often.*

As to the directory, I favor either of two methods: a simple address book or a file of 3" X 5" cards. Both have the advantage of being easily replaceable, since there are now address books with replacement sections. However, there are advantages to a 3x5 card file. Computers or hand-held electronic devices may also be used.

I favor copying all the names, addresses and phone numbers onto 3X5 cards and keeping them in a little file box. At the bottom of the cards, or on the backs, write in any information about the people that you may want to remember. For instance, if couples have children, write in the names and birth dates of the children. If you need directions to someone's house, write the directions on the back of the card. Then, copy the entire card, front and back, and take one of the two cards with you if you are going to their home. That means you have their address, phone number, and directions with you when you may need them, and if you misplace the card you travel with, you still have one on file. Another thing you can do with duplicate cards is to file them under different letters. So, If a person whose last name begins with "R" is your insurance agent, file one card under "R" and one under "I" for "insurance." And, of course, when it is time to send someone a birthday or anniversary card, you can always find their address.

Once you have a useable directory and a chart showing all the occasions you want to commemorate with a card, the next thing you need is a supply of all-purpose cards. Why all-purpose cards? Julie's account will explain:

I love to let people know that I am thinking of them on special occasions like birthdays and anniversaries, and I like to pick out special cards just to suit them. However, things happened to make me re-think some of that. First, when I knew someone's special day was coming, I would plan a trip to a card shop, but sometimes it was not convenient. I would end up missing the occasion, and have to get one of those "belated" cards, or just skip sending the card altogether.

A second problem was time. It would sometimes take me fifteen or twenty minutes to pick out the perfect card. Add to that ten minutes to the shop and ten minutes back, and you have a 35 or 40 minute chunk of time dedicated to one card. In a month in which there were six or eight occasions, I would end up investing a great deal of time.

A third problem was money. When I was a graduate student, time and money were at a premium, and the prices of the better greeting cards just keep going up! It seems as though yesterday that I could get a good card for 95 cents. Now it is more like three dollars and ninety-five cents, or even more! I just could not handle the expense when I was a graduate student, and I still have trouble with it now.

Between the problems of time and expense, my performance on sending greeting cards to persons I care about was going downhill fast. Then the author challenged me to examine some of the assumptions I was making. Most importantly, he asked me if the quality of the card were truly important, or if the fact of my thinking enough about a person to mail a card - any card - on time was the important point. I decided to act on his advice and try something. I went to a card shop and bought a pack of all-purpose greeting cards. They had an artist's pleasant rendition of an ocean beach on the front, and nothing whatsoever inside. They cost me four dollars for a box of twenty (twenty cents each). I kept them in my desk drawer. Every time I would check the chart that I had made at the author's suggestion, and would find a birthday or an anniversary coming up, I would write the appropriate message inside and send the card. It was inexpensive and convenient. I was a bit scared at first that someone would think me cheap for sending that kind of card, but compliments started coming in from people who sounded very happy that I remembered them. I even asked a few of them point blank: "Were you offended by the type of card I sent?" They seemed confused by the question. It apparently just did not register with them that I had made a birthday or anniversary card out of a generic card. They also said it meant more to them to find an actual card in their mailbox than it would have to have received an eCard. Am I glad I listened to advice on this issue! Because of the convenience of this system, I'm remembering more people than ever before, and with a very manageable expenditure of time and money.

A Few Words of Caution in the Electronic Age

We are in the age of computers, cell phones, smart phones, social media and text messaging. It is far beyond the scope of this book to provide guidance on matters such as how to best set up email groups and on whether and how best to manage social media sites such as Facebook and Twitter. However, I will offer two cautionary notes.

Once it is out there, it is out there!

Once you join a social media site, you have to be aware that anyone could gain access to your posts. This includes potential employers, college and graduate school admissions committees, professional boards, et cetera. Your posts and pictures may have unintended consequences. I know of an instance in which a woman who wanted to work as a yoga instructor was in the habit of posting pictures of herself. Most of her pictures showed her holding a bottle of beer in her hand. She applied for a job at a Yoga studio, and the manager of the studio looked her up on Facebook. When the manager saw that the majority of the person's pictures showed her holding a bottle of beer, she decided that this was not the image she wanted portrayed of her Yoga studio. The individual was turned down for the job.

That was actually a rather benign consequence of a person's Facebook posts. She simply lost out on one particular job opportunity. In current professional psychology workshops on ethics and legal issues, it has come to light that serious ethical issues can result from injudicious posts. It is advisable, before you make social media posts, to ask yourself, "Could the information I am intending to share put me in an unfavorable light in any important situation?" Proceed with caution.

Text messaging: When is it enough?

"In the old days," before cell phones and text messaging, people were out of contact with one another for hours, sometimes days, at a time. If you think of human civilization as starting at the time of the first written records, we have had about 6,000 years of human civilization. Cell phones have been in common use for about one-quarter of one percent of that time, and text messaging is even more recent. We got by quite adequately, perhaps even better, when we were temporarily out of touch.

There are certainly many terrific advantages of cell phones. However, there are drawbacks, and I will add a note of caution about a few of them.

In my work, I listen to and respond to an enormous number of re-lationship issues. In many instances, I have had patients sit in my office, take out their cell phones, and read to me a long array of texts between themselves and their relationship partners. My pa-tients are frequently upset about the meaning, or supposed "tone" of a text. Please remember, when you are talking with someone face-to-face, you see a great deal of body language: posture, ges-tures, and facial expressions. In addition to the words you hear, there are vocal qualities: volume, cadence, tone and inflections. In a text message, all the vocal qualities and all the body language are absent. This is a medium ripe for misunderstandings.

A second problem text messaging can cause in relationships is that it upsets the balance between your life with your partner and your life away from your partner. In general, the healthiest relation-ships appear to be those in which partners invest about half of their time and their overall life energy to the relationship. They invest the other half of their time and life energy to education, career, friendships, and pastimes that do not directly include the partner.

By investing half their emotional resources to activities outside the relationship, each partner experiences growth. They acquire knowledge, skills and resources that they then bring back to the relationship. This strengthens the relationship in two ways. First, they make themselves even more desirable through their growth. Second, by combining the knowledge, skills and resources that each of them has acquired outside the relationship, they make themselves stronger and more resourceful as a couple.

Frequent or constant texting back and forth, day after day, is a practice of many couples in today's electronic age. There is a danger in this frequent, if not constant, focus on the partner. It may detract from the psychological energy available to derive growth from, or even succeed at, independent activities. Use text messaging judiciously

There is a third problem that I have seen with text messaging. It appears to be obscuring normal boundary issues, and to encourage less socially conscious attitudes. If you saw a friend of yours sitting at a table with their father or mother at a restaurant, you would probably not walk up, pull up a chair, sit down, and say, "Do you want to see a movie tonight?" That behavior would be crossing an invisible boundary, and most people would see it as socially inappropriate. You would usually respect your friend's right and their parent's right to their time together, and you would not intrude. However, the advent of texting appears to be eliminating awareness of social boundaries, since we can text anytime, anywhere. There appears to be a growing sense that we have the right to enter another person's world without any normal context that would make it seem appropriate. The effect on boundary awareness may be subtle, but it is nonetheless one that bears scrutiny. Again, use text messaging judiciously.

CHAPTER 27

ENTERTAINING IN THE HOME

Why does it seem so difficult?

The feeling of being connected to other people is one of the experiences that make life satisfying and enjoyable. Sharing leisure time with people who mean something to us is a time-honored custom, and entertaining others in our own homes is a fine way of doing so. There are, however, a number of factors typical of modern life that discourage people from entertaining in their homes. Two are particularly relevant:

1. Time

Nowadays, in the majority of families, two adults work outside the home. This reduces the time and energy available for planning and carrying out home entertainment. In addition, many people believe that to be suitable for entertaining, their home must be in a state of order and cleanliness that they rarely achieve during their daily lives. I have heard a number of persons remark that they put off plans to entertain because they do not want to face the task of making their home "presentable."

2. Money

During the ten years from 1980 to 1990, only ten percent of American families gained in the buying power of their income. An additional ten percent stayed the same, and fully eighty percent of American families actually lost buying power during the decade. The situation has grown worse in subsequent decades. If you believe that entertaining friends or relatives will be an expensive endeavor, you may avoid it for financial reasons.

If considerations of time and money keep you from entertaining people in your home, then you are missing a wonderful opportunity to have fun and to make and deepen social contacts. When you entertain in your home, there are typically fewer distractions than there are in public places. You are more in control of the environment, and may have more time and privacy. Home-based social events can be more easy-going, lighthearted and fun. They can afford opportunity to share ideas, opinions, feelings, and values. It would be a shame to let issues of time and money prevent you from entertaining at home!

As far as the time needed to maintain the home in a state suitable for receiving guests, I hope that the suggestions in chapter 19 will help you, with minimal effort, to maintain your home so that its normal state is acceptable. Furthermore, you may have to challenge your own belief that your home has to be in perfect shape in order to be acceptable for guests. It is as though we all go around conspiring with one another to maintain a deception. When you have made a special effort to make your home more clean and orderly than usual to receive guests, you must realize that your guests are perceptive enough to know that that state of order is not typical for you. Moreover, when you visit people who have made a similar effort, you know that you are not seeing their home in its natural state. If you can agree with the people with whom you socialize not to go on with that collusion, perhaps you can all accept a reasonable level of neatness and more easily face the tasks associated with entertaining.

The Sunday Brunch

As for the expense, try entertaining people on Sunday mornings for brunch. A Sunday brunch has a number of advantages, including the following:

1. Reasonable Expense: Breakfast foods are not very expensive. Eggs, breads, and fruit can make up the core of the Sunday brunch menu. I have given over 60 Sunday brunches over the years, and at today's prices it can be done very well for approximately three dollars per person.

2. Relaxing Time: First, you and your guests have had Saturday to take care of many of the tasks and obligations left over from the workweek. Second, at a brunch starting at 10:30 a.m. most people will have a more relaxed energy state than they would have at a late night party. Evening parties sometimes cause people to experience a more frenetic energy, perhaps to battle sleepiness. The social atmosphere at a brunch is typically very pleasant.

3. Opportunity for New or Renewed Contacts: While most guests may leave by 1:00 p.m. from a brunch that starts at 10:30 a.m., a few with whom you are having particularly good rapport may stay around. This affords an opportunity to get to know new people better and to renew or deepen established friendships.

4. Avoid the clean-up blues: You will have plenty of time and energy to clean up after a brunch. In contrast it is more difficult to face a post-party mess at 2:00 a.m.

I hope that these ideas on Sunday brunches will prove helpful. Try it. You may find that the Sunday brunch opens up a completely new era of home entertainment for you.

Theme Dinners with Shared Work and Expense

Another idea for affordable and relatively easy home entertainment is a variation on the "pot luck supper." My version is similar to pot luck in that persons or couples attending are asked to bring something to serve, but there are two major differences. First, instead of being completely "left to luck," the dinner selections are structured around a theme. Second, there are usually a limited number of invited guests, and there is some ongoing discussion between the time of first invitation and the dinner. Thus, there is an implied commitment to keep the date and participate, the menu is much more orchestrated than it would be in a true "pot luck," and there is occasion to make contact during the days leading up to the dinner. I have thought up and tried all the theme dinners that will be described below, some of them many times. You may want to try them, too.

Garlic Fest: Obviously, this is a dinner to which all the guests bring a dish featuring garlic. An exception may be made for a fruity or "cooling" dessert or relish. The following are some of the dishes I have encountered at garlic fests:

• • • shrimp scampi

• • • white lasagna with garlic and oil

• • • salad with toasted, minced garlic

• • • garlic soup

• • • garlic bread

• • • chicken sautéed in garlic

• • • spaghetti "aglio ed olio" (served with fresh garlic, minced and sautéed in olive oil)

It adds to the fun of a garlic fest if people think up some intriguing dishes to bring. The jokes about how no one else will want to come near us for a week are inevitable.

Plebeian Night: The word "plebeian" comes from the word "plebes" which is the ancient Roman term for commoners. It means common, or even coarse or low. However, Plebeian Night is *not* intended to be coarse or low, but rather to be creative and entertaining. When invited for "Plebeian Night," participants are asked to start with an ordinary, down-to-earth, plebeian dish, but to find some way to make it more elaborate or tasty, while maintaining the basic recipe. These "guidelines" usually result in a fair amount of communication back and forth during the week or two leading up to Plebeian Night. People ask what others are bringing and often ask for suggestions. This contributes to the social life that the event creates, and to the fun of the event itself.

The following are a few of the dishes I have eaten at Plebeian Night:
• • • tuna and noodle casserole (see Appendix C for the recipe).
• • • macaroni & cheese with diced olives and water chestnuts.
• • • baked beans with mint seasoning
• • • jello (fruit mold)
• • • American chop suey with diced onions, peppers, olives, and water chestnuts
• • • baked apples

Other theme dinners I have hosted are Italian Night, Mexican Night, and Seafood Night, none of which require any explanation. Here are a few suggestions for planning theme dinners:

1. Tentatively decide on a theme, a date, and a guest list. Do this at least 3 weeks before your chosen date. Saturday can be a better night than Friday for this type of event, since it gives participants all day Saturday to prepare.
2. Call people to ask if they are interested and see if enough people are available on your chosen date.
3. Singles and couples are fine. Everyone should be willing to contribute to the menu.
4. Keep in touch with your participants even after they have accepted. Ask them what they intend to bring. Try to orchestrate things to some extent so as to avoid duplication, but be flexible. Remember that it is the occasion that is of most importance, not the balance of the menu. Tell people what others are intending to bring. Often, some pre-event communication is generated.
5. If participants ask you if there is anything else they can bring, be willing to say "yes." Whether it is ice cubes, drinks, mixers, napkins, paper plates, or bread, there are bound to be items that need to be provided. Say "yes" to at least some offers in order to keep your own responsibilities manageable. For a theme night, *you are a facilitator, not the one and only provider.*
6. At the dinner, if you are happy with the mix of guests and the feeling of the occasion, ask participants if they want to do it again, with another theme. It is possible that you will end up with a core group of people who will take turns hosting theme nights. It is a fine way to generate enthusiasm for a continuing series of social occasions during an era in which home entertaining is on the decline. This could really give a boost to your social life, and it can all be done with shared work and expense! Enjoy!

APPENDIX A

STIMULUS QUESTIONNAIRE

This stimulus questionnaire has approximately 50 items organized into 8 sections. Read each item and then circle the number which best represents your reaction, as follows:

1 definite yes
2 yes
3 no
4 definite no

Be aware of your thoughts and feelings, and any images that come to mind as you read and answer the items. Next, look over your answers. Notice whether your strongest reactions are spread throughout the questionnaire or are concentrated in a few areas. This will give you a clue as to which sections and chapters in the book will be of most interest to you.

After you have read the book, go through the questionnaire again, and see if any of your responses have changed. This type of informal self-appraisal will help you to make sure you are managing your life in ways that make you feel happy and competent.

1. <u>VALUES AND LIFE GOALS</u>

I am satisfied with my achievements   1   2   3   4

I fear that I am not making progress toward a
long term goal or dream.   1   2   3   4

I know I would like my life to be different in five
years, but I am not sure in what way or how to
work toward the change.   1   2   3   4

As I consider a. AWARENESS, b. HAPPINESS,
c. PRODUCTIVITY, d. MEANING, and
e. RELATEDNESS; I rate them, in order of their
importance to me, as follows:

_____ AWARENESS ___MEANING
_____PRODUCTIVITY

_____HAPPINESS   _____RELATEDNESS

2.   MOTIVATION AND EMOTIONAL FACTORS

I am my own most severe critic.   1   2   3   4

I evaluate my self-worth on basis of my
competence and achievements.   1   2   3   4

I go through periods of the blues in which my
productivity falls off significantly for
days at a time.   1   2   3   4

I lose the enjoyment of listening to music or
watching a movie because my mind
drifts off to work-related issues.   1   2   3   4

After significant achievements, I feel
more relief than joy.   1   2   3   4

Sometimes I get so caught up in tasks that I
end up wondering what I am doing it all for.
    1   2   3   4

3.   MANAGING STRESS AND STRAIN

I keep thinking about tasks that I have not
done.   1   2   3   4

I have so many things to do that I cannot seem
to concentrate on any one.   1   2   3   4

I often feel tired or tense due to not enough sleep.
    1   2   3   4

I would be able to relax better if I exercised more.

                                             1   2   3   4

I get headaches when I am under stress.

            1   2   3   4

My jaw sometimes feels tense or clenched.

            1   2   3   4

Sometimes my neck and shoulders get
stiff or sore from being tense.   1   2   3   4

When I do relax I realize how tense I've been.

            1   2   3   4

I rarely listen closely to music because
I am thinking too much.   1   2   3   4

I get disappointed when I lose a game.

            1   2   3   4

4.   TIME AND TASK MANAGEMENT

I like to keep a written agenda to remind me of
tasks that I wish to accomplish.   1   2   3   4

I detest lists of tasks.   1   2   3   4

I don't like to keep lists, but I resort to it
during periods of high demand.   1   2   3   4

I am most productive when I maintain
a consistent routine.   1   2   3   4

I procrastinate when a task seems so massive
that I cannot easily see where to begin.
                                     1   2   3   4

I fail to send birthday or anniversary cards
because I don't remember the dates.
                                     1   2   3   4

I am aware of the times of day during which I am
capable of my best concentration and work.
                                     1   2   3   4

I find myself trying to remember names or
trying to find frequently-used phone numbers.
                                     1   2   3   4

It would help if I would keep a calendar to record
tax exempt expenditures, birthdays, reminders
for car maintenance, etc.   1   2   3   4

While trying to straighten out business
situations, I wish I had written down names
and dates of prior contracts.   1   2   3   4

5.   MATERIALS /PHYSICAL ENVIRONMENT

I think that a neat desk is a sign of an
uncreative mind.   1   2   3   4

I like to use file folders and bulletin boards.
             1   2   3   4

File folders and bulletin boards and I
do not get along.
             1   2   3   4

I have some material possessions (e.g. car,
boat, sporting equipment) about which I feel
uncomfortable because I neglect maintenance.
             1   2   3   4

My desk, office, or work space seems to me
to be cluttered and inconvenient.   1   2   3   4

The clutter in my living or work space builds up
because I think it will be so difficult to organize it.
             1   2   3   4

6. PERSONAL FINANCE

I have put money away, intending to use it for
a special purpose, only to have it "disappear into
my cash flow" so that I can no longer find that
money when I want it.   1   2   3   4

I have gone on vacation, and have felt guilty
about the expenditures I was making.
                                    1   2   3   4

I have agonized over spending money because
I wondered if some expense might be coming
up, like an insurance premium or a car repair.
                                    1   2   3   4

I would like to save or invest money for my future,
but I cannot seem to put enough money aside to
do so.   1   2   3   4

I have made adequate financial plans for my
retirement.   1   2   3   4

7. EXERCISE

I am just about as physically fit as I wish to be.
                                    1   2   3   4

My physical workouts lose out in competition
with other obligations.   1   2   3   4

I like working out once I get started, but I resist getting started in the first place.   1   2   3   4

Once I am into a workout routine, I start increasing the routine until it feels burdensome
                                      1   2   3   4

I do not like any physical exercise that is not fun.
                                 1   2   3   4

Noontime might be a good time to exercise. But I am unwilling to give up lunch time as a time to socialize.   1   2   3   4

8. SOCIAL AND FAMILY LIFE

I have friends and relatives to whom I wish I
would write more often.   1   2   3   4

I would like to entertain people in my home, but
I am afraid I will not do it well enough.
    1   2   3   4

I would like to entertain people in my home, but
it seems to be too expensive.   1   2   3   4

I forget to send greeting cards on birthdays and
anniversaries, and I feel badly when I do.
    1   2   3   4

I have difficulty finding friends who share
my special interests.   1   2   3   4

If I have not written to someone in awhile, I feel
that nothing but a long letter will do. Since
writing a long letter seems tedious, the
situation perpetuates itself.   1   2   3   4

APPENDIX B

Birthdays & Anniversaries

January	July
February	**August**
March	**September**

April	October
May	November
June	December

APPENDIX C

A Recipe for "Plebeian Night"

Tuna and Noodle Casserole

<u>Ingredients</u>
2 cans white tuna
1 can sliced water chestnuts
½ cup carrots, diced
½ cup onion, diced
½ cup celery, diced
1 lb. egg noodles
¾ cup Swiss cheese, grated
2 slices whole wheat bread
2 cans cream of celery soup
1 cup milk
2 teaspoons basil or oregano

<u>Directions</u>

Grate up the Swiss cheese. Crumble up the two slices of whole wheat bread, and mix the breadcrumbs and cheese together. Set this mixture aside.

Put the egg noodles in to boil, and take note of the time needed to cook them.

Heat up the two cans of cream of celery soup with a cup of milk, and add the oregano or basil.
When there are 4 minutes left, add the diced celery to the egg noodles. When there are 3 minutes left, add the diced onions and carrots to the egg noodles.

Drain the mixture of egg noodles, celery, onions and carrots in a colander.

Mix together the egg noodles/vegetables with the sauce and place this mixture in a casserole dish.

Crumble the tuna and spread it over the top. Spread the sliced water chestnuts over the top.

Spread the Swiss cheese/bread crumb mixture on top.
Dot with butter.

Bake for 30-35 minutes at 325-350 degrees.

Enjoy! What was once a plebeian dish is now a delightful entrée.

APPENDIX D

GLOSSARY

anxiety

An uneasy, uncomfortable feeling in the absence of a clear, identifiable threat. Emotional anxiety is often accompanied by physical tension, and is distinguished from fear, in which an identifiable threat is present.

blues

See "depressed mood."

compulsive

Of or pertaining to a compulsion. A compulsion in psychology is usually thought of as the anxiety-driven performance or repetition of a behavior. Compulsive behavior falls along a continuum. At one end of the continuum are efficient, organized task-completion methods that are beneficial in that they increase an individual's comfort, safety, or productivity and that are not associated with undue anxiety. At the other end of the continuum are behaviors that are so overdone or detailed that they are not beneficial, and that are associated with undue anxiety. At the former end of the continuum, compulsive behavior is a character trait; at the latter end, it is a disorder.

congruence

In geometry, congruence denotes the exact similarity of geometric shapes. The late and famous psychologist Carl Rogers used the word to denote the compatibility of a person's inner experience and outward behavior.

depressed mood

A symptom, typically characterized by sadness, loss of humor, loss of pleasure in usual pastimes, and loss of feelings of competence and well-being.

depression

A disorder, often including depressed mood. The syndrome of depression, called "major depression," can be a biologically self-perpetuating state of being, signaled by symptoms such as disturbances of sleep and appetite, psychomotor agitation or slowing, and loss of energy and sexual desire.

dream

In this volume there is no discussion of dreams in the sense of a series of images, ideas, and emotions occurring during sleep.

There is considerable discussion of dreams as deeply held hopes or ambitions. An assumption is made that many individuals maintain conscious hopes and ambitions that become part of their self-definition. If impetus for achieving dreams diminishes with time, it could be an unfortunate loss. This book encourages the idea of keeping dreams alive in order to enhance vital, purposeful, committed living.

existentialism

A philosophical movement associated with Jean-Paul Sartre and others. Existentialists seek a heightened awareness of actual existence, and emphasize issues of self-determination, freedom, death, isolation, and meaning.

extremities

Those parts of the body, such as the hands, feet, and head, that are furthest from the heart. These body parts have a high proportion of surface area to volume, and thus are efficient radiators of body heat.

goal

Typically defined as the purpose or end toward which an endeavor is directed. In this volume, there is an implicit assumption that personal goals are determined in the context of values, needs, and preferences.

In addition, in some treatments of the topic, steps toward goals are defined as "objectives." However, in this volume, "objectives" and "goals" are roughly synonymous, and "steps toward goals" are called exactly that.

imperatives

Words and expressions that denote a rigid, absolutistic interpretation of events. Words and expressions such as "should, ought, must, and have to" can have a powerful effect on human emotions, and are often used as premises leading to irrationality. (See "irrational thinking").

initial insomnia

Difficulty or delay in falling asleep.

internal monitoring

In this volume, this expression is used to denote any method by which an individual reminds h/self of tasks or obligations by the use of a memory technique. The technique can allow a person to be responsible in addressing important obligations with de creased use of calendars, lists, appointment books, or hand-held electronic devices.

irrational thinking

Thinking characterized by logic that begins with an unsupportable premise. For instance, if we start with the premise that to be successful we must be competent at every endeavor, then if we fail at one thing we can logically deduce that we are not successful. Although the deduction is logical, the premise is flawed since it cannot be proven that competence at everything is a requirement of success. Irrational thinking is a very frequent cause of human discomfort, and even misery.

kinesthetic

Also known as the "proprioceptive sense," this is the sense that allows us to know the position of our body in space and to be aware of motion. Often, the tactile sense is included, and the word "kinesthetic" is understood in this volume to denote all the feeling senses.

mastery

The act or feeling of being competent or in control. Mastery has been seen as a basic human need since the work of Sigmund Freud's student and colleague Alfred Adler. In this volume, the word mastery is used to denote a moderate, healthy degree of competence and control.

mental imagery

A process by which persons represent the external world in their internal consciousness. Mental imagery may occur in all sense modalities (visual, auditory, tactile, kinesthetic, olfactory, and gustatory), and may be thought of as a bridge between the external world and abstract thought.

motivation

Motivation is usually thought of simply as the desire to achieve something. In this volume, there will be a distinction drawn between "plain motivation" and "effective motivation." The latter term implies that motivation consists of six components:

1. setting a goal
2. breaking the goal down into achievable steps
3. overcoming external barriers to goal attainment
4. overcoming internal barriers to goal attainment
5. seeking help when appropriate
6. anticipating future rewards

negative self talk

This term denotes the process of reminding oneself that unfavorable outcomes are possible. Potentially self-defeating, negative self-talk is **not** necessarily irrational, in that unfavorable outcomes are indeed possible. Negative self-talk can lead to irrational thinking. If you not only recognize the possibility of unfavorable circumstances, but go on to say you will "not be able to stand" those circumstances, you have moved to irrational thinking. (See "irrational thinking").

personal growth

This is a frequently used term in the fields of counseling and psychology, and is rather nebulous. In this volume, the term may be thought of as the process of enhancing one's effective pursuit of awareness, joy, productivity, meaning, or relationships.

progressive relaxation

A technique for the reduction of physiological tension. This method was first developed in the western world by the physiologist

Edmund Jacobson and later shortened to an easily usable technique by the psychologist Joseph Wolpe, Richard Suinn and others. The technique provides a remarkably effective means for persons to beneficially alter their physical state of being. The technique is characterized by a series of non-strenuous physical exercises in which the individual first tenses and then releases different muscle groups throughout the body. The individual focuses attention on the difference between tense feelings and relaxed feelings, and learns to let muscle tension decrease. The method is often enhanced by certain ways of focusing attention, and by deep breathing and imagery.

psychotherapy

A treatment process by which a practitioner, usually a psychologist, social worker, or professional counselor, helps a client to attain increased comfort, adjustment, and happiness through a verbal form of therapy. Psychotherapy typically focuses on the client's thoughts, feelings, memories, behaviors, and relationships. There is a very wide variety of theories and methods currently in use. However, ethical standards are almost always very similar, and are designed to ensure a high quality of service and to protect clients' rights to confidentiality.

slump

In this volume, the word "slump" will be used to denote a period of depressed mood in which a person finds it difficult to maintain his or her typical level of energy and productivity.

stress

In physics, a stress refers to a force applied to a material. In this volume, stress refers to any environmental change to which a human being must react. Thus, any stimulation is stress. However, stress will usually be discussed in terms of expectations, obligations and tasks.

strain

In physics, strain denotes the rearrangement of molecules in a material due to a stress. In this volume, strain refers to human responses to stress. Specifically, strain includes physical tension, emotional anxiety, disruption of habits, irrational thinking, and loss of pleasure.

stressor

An expectation, obligation, or demand impinging on a person. The word "stressor" is sometimes used to emphasize that it refers to a force acting on a person from an external source.

tension

A constellation of physiological events, experienced as the specific discomfort of muscle tension. Physical tension is typically accompanied by changes in every major system of the body. It includes faster heart rate and breathing, elevated blood pressure, increased sweating, increased secretion of acids in the stomach and adrenalin-related substances into the bloodstream, immune system suppression, and increased electro-chemical activity in the nervous tissue. Most persons can be taught to decrease tension through methods such as progressive relaxation exercises.

terminal insomnia

Usually known as "early morning awakening," this is a symptom in which an individual awakens hours before his or her normal rising time and is unable to fall back asleep.

time management

Improved efficiency in the use of time, leading to increased productivity relative to time allotted.

value

verb: To assign a degree of importance to.

noun: An abstract principle, quality, ideal, or attribute that is considered important. In this volume, only abstract nouns are considered to be values. Thus, although a person may value a car, "car" is **not** a value. Abstractions that a car may represent, such as freedom or convenience, are values.

About the Author

Michael Slavit is a psychologist in private practice. He received his Bachelor's degree in Psychology at Brown University, his Master's degree in Counseling at the University of Rhode Island and his Doctorate in Counseling Psychology at the University of Texas at Austin. He is board certified in Cognitive and Behavioral Psychology by the American Board of Professional Psychology. However, he considers his most important credential to be the confidence of his patients.

Dr. Slavit's past positions have included Assistant Professor of Counseling and Human Development Services at the University of Georgia and Director of Counseling at Southern College of Technology.

Dr. Slavit treats patients for a variety of issues including depression, anxiety, ADHD, unresolved grief, relationship issues, and health/fitness/weight. He believes that not all personal problems have to be viewed as emotional disorders, but may often be more appropriately seen as inevitable problems adjusting happily to a complex and demanding world. Dr. Slavit has produced over a hundred handouts and brochures to help educate his patients, and is the author of *Cure Your Money Ills: Improve Your Self-esteem through Personal Budgeting* and *Lessons from Desiderata*. He has works in process, including books on embracing fitness and coping with ADHD.

APPENDIX E

REFERENCES

American Heritage Dictionary . 2nd College Edition. Boston: Houghton Mifflin (1982).

Bernstein, D. And Borkovec, T. *Progressive Relaxation Training.* Champaign, IL: Research Press (1973).

Ellis, Albert and Harper, Robert. *A New Guide to Rational Living.* North Hollywood, CA: Wilshire Books (1978).

Jacobson, Edmund. *You Must Relax.* New York: McGraw-Hill (1934).

Jacobson, Edmund. *Progressive Relaxation.* Chicago: University of Chicago Press (1938).

Jacobson, Edmund, "The origins and development of progressive relaxation," *Journal of Behavior Therapy and Experimental Psychiatry,* 1977, 8: 119-123.

Johnson, E. & McClelland, D. *Learning to Achieve.* Glenview: IL: Scott, Foresman and Co., 1984.

Johnson, Mark A. *The Random Walk and Beyond : An Inside Guide to the Stock Market* . New York: John Wiley (1988).

Kline, Nathan. *From Sad to Glad*. New York: Ballantine Books (1974).

Lakein, Alan. *How to Get Control of Your Time and Your Life*. New York: The New American Library (1973).

O'Neil, William J. *How to Make Money in Stocks*. New York: McGraw-Hill (1988).

Paul, Gordon L., "Physiological effects of relaxation training and hypnotic suggestion," *Journal of Abnormal Psychology*, 1969, 74: 425-437.

Slavit, Michael R. *The Effects of Assessing and Utilizing Preferred Sensory Modality: An Experiment with Relaxation Training*. Doctoral Dissertation. University of Texas, 1983.

Slavit, Michael R. *CURE YOUR MONEY ILLS: Enhance Your Self Esteem through Personal Budgeting*. Saratoga, CA: R&E Publishers (1992).

Smith, Manuel J. *When I Say No I Feel Guilty*. New York: Dial Press (1975).

Tufts University Diet and Nutrition Letter, Vol. 10, No. 4, June 1992.

Wayner, Stephen A. *Buying Right: Getting Started in Real Estate Investment*. New York: Franklin Watts (1987).

Willis, Clint, "How to make sure your money lasts your lifetime," *Money*, Vol. 20, No. 6, June, 1991.

Wolpe, Joseph. *Psychotherapy by Reciprocal Inhibition*. Palo Alto, CA: Stanford University Press (1958).

Yarnell, Thomas G., "Five keys to greater self-motivation," *Piedmont Airlines Magazine*, June 1985.

18257485R00135

Made in the USA
Middletown, DE
01 March 2015